职业教育·航空运输类专业教材

Minhang Chengwu Yingyu
民航乘务英语

主　编　潘国强
副主编　裘海璇　徐　冉

人民交通出版社
北　京

内 容 提 要

本书为职业教育航空运输类专业教材。全书共分8个单元，其中第1~7单元主要围绕乘机和机上旅客服务的流程进行设计，第8单元主要关于空乘求职与面试。为帮助学习者了解、学习客舱服务的广播用语，在附录中收集整理了客舱服务中常用的广播词。

本书具有两大特点：一是在内容设计上，突出场景再现与技能应用，将空乘的职业英语能力融入空乘一线岗位的工作与服务过程，旨在通过场景再现习得语言技能并加以提高巩固；二是在内容编排上，不但每个单元均设计了听、说、读、写练习，以便英语综合技能的提高，同时还设计了课前热身、填词游戏等练习，以增加课程教学的趣味性和提高学生学习积极性。

本书适合职业院校空中乘务专业使用，也可作为航空公司在职人员或从事外航服务的人员使用。

本书配有教学课件和外教对话音频，读者可加入QQ群"职教轨道教学研讨群（群号：129327355）"获取。

图书在版编目（CIP）数据

民航乘务英语/潘国强主编.—北京:人民交通出版社股份有限公司，2024.8
　　ISBN 978-7-114-19444-3

Ⅰ.①民…　Ⅱ.①潘…　Ⅲ.①民用航空—乘务人员—英语　Ⅳ.①F560.9

中国国家版本馆CIP数据核字(2024)第055701号

职业教育·航空运输类专业教材

书　　　名：民航乘务英语
著　作　者：潘国强
责任编辑：于　涛
责任校对：赵媛媛　魏佳宁
责任印制：刘高彤
出版发行：人民交通出版社
地　　　址：（100011）北京市朝阳区安定门外外馆斜街3号
网　　　址：http://www.ccpcl.com.cn
销售电话：（010）59757973
总　经　销：人民交通出版社发行部
经　　　销：各地新华书店
印　　　刷：北京建宏印刷有限公司
开　　　本：787×1092　1/16
印　　　张：8
字　　　数：256千
版　　　次：2024年8月　第1版
印　　　次：2024年8月　第1次印刷
书　　　号：ISBN 978-7-114-19444-3
定　　　价：32.00元

（有印刷、装订质量问题的图书，由本社负责调换）

前言 PREFACE

　　空乘学生职业英语水平的高低直接关系到能否被航空公司录用以及后续自身的发展空间。一本既适合教师"教"，又适合学生"学"的空乘英语教材是帮助学生提高职业英语水平，实现蓝天梦想的重要保障。

　　相较于传统的空乘英语教材，本教材在内容设计上更突出职业性和场景性，以实用和够用为原则，通过职业场景再现，模拟乘机流程及客舱服务，将语言习得与技能提高融入职业环境；在内容编排上，更强调循序渐进和听说读写的综合性，每个单元均以课前热身开始，并综合设计了听说读写等环节，以便学生英语综合水平的提高；在项目设计上摒弃乏味且容易使学生产生挫败感的长篇阅读理解，通过一个个精心设计的小任务、小挑战，激发学生的学习兴趣和积极性，使学生在获得体验感的同时在不知不觉中提高英语水平。

　　本教材由浙江交通职业技术学院潘国强担任主编，负责全书的结构设计并负责统稿。教材具体编写分工如下：浙江交通职业技术学院裘海璇负责编写Unit 2、Unit 4、Unit 6和Unit 7，中法航空大学徐冉负责编写Unit 1、Unit 3、Unit 5和Unit 8，潘国强负责编写整理附录客舱服务广播词。编写过程中浙江交通职业技术学院曹文瀛和姚璐艳两位老师给予了许多好的建议，在此表示感谢。

　　书中部分图片取自互联网相关网站，特此鸣谢。由于编者水平有限，书中疏漏不妥之处在所难免，恳请同行及读者不吝指正。

作　者

2023年5月

CONTENTS 目录

Unit 1	Pre-flight and Boarding	1
Unit 2	Routines after Take-off	11
Unit 3	Passenger Comfort	20
Unit 4	Food and Drinks Service	31
Unit 5	Health and Medical Issues	42
Unit 6	Safety and Emergencies	53
Unit 7	Descent, Landing and Layover	62
Unit 8	Getting a Job	71
Appendix	Announcement for Practice	80
Glossary		88
Audio Script		95
Answer Key		109

Unit 1 Pre-flight and Boarding

TAXI

1. Warm-up: discuss in pairs and answer the following questions.

I. What is the situation in the picture?

II. What do you think is the cause of such a situation? How can the cabin crew cope with it?

III. Complete the crossword puzzle with the given words and clues.

ACROSS	DOWN
(3) You pack your things in your_____ when traveling. (5) You wear your_____ to listen to music. (6) You have to_____ if the passengers have fastened their seatbelts before take-off. (8) You give another person the_____ by telling him to go left or right. (9) The space inside a plane.	(1) Toilet. (2) You give a safety_____ before take-off. (4) Before the flight. (6)The_____ is always crowded when passengers are boarding. (7) Say hi to others.

earphone　　greet　　　　check　　　cabin　　　　corridor
pre-flight　　lavatory　　luggage　　direction　　demonstration

2. Spot: what pre-flight task is the cabin crew member in each picture doing?

A. giving away earphones　　　　　B. giving safety demonstrations
C. greeting passengers　　　　　　 D. showing seats
E. cabin check　　　　　　　　　　F. helping passengers with hand luggage

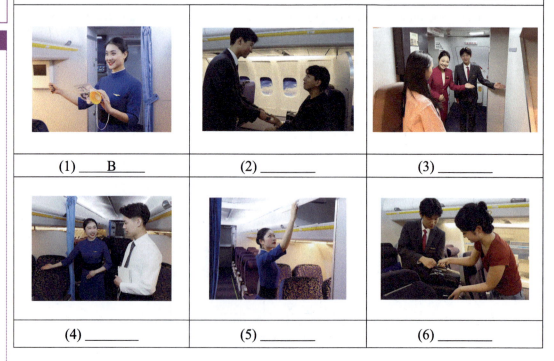

| (1) ___B___ | (2) _____ | (3) _____ |
| (4) _____ | (5) _____ | (6) _____ |

3. Brainstorm: what other jobs will flight attendants have before take-off?

e.g. Briefing passengers at the emergency exit.

4. Converse: choose one of the jobs from task 3 and role-play with a partner. Try to use the following sentence patterns.

Giving away things: Sir/Madam, this is your_____. Here you are.
Checking things: How can I help, sir/madam?
Helping with things: Please let me help.

5. Greet: how to greet these passengers?

I. How to address and greet the passengers in pictures ①-④? Choose from the following greetings (more than one options may apply).

Greeting A: Morning! How do you do?
Greeting B: Hello dear. Welcome on board.
Greeting C: Good morning, sir/madam. Good to see you again.
Greeting D: Welcome on board. Do you need any help, madam?

II. It is important to identify what problems passengers might have during boarding. Discuss with your partner: what difficulties might these passengers have?

Passenger problems: e.g. carrying heavy luggage.

TAKE-OFF

6. Directions and seats.

I. How to explain the location of the marked seats (from A to H)? Try to give directions with the given expressions.

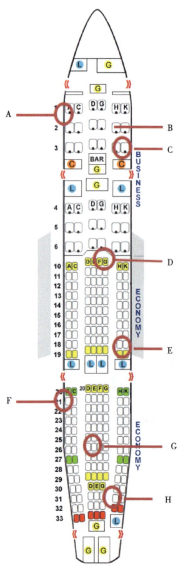

DIRECTIONS

on the left/right	by the lavatory
at the front/end	by the emergency exit
in the middle	the first/second/.../last row
down the aisle/corridor	window/aisle seat

SHOWING SEATS

Welcome on board. Can I have a look at your boarding pass, please?

Your seat is this way.

You'll find your seat there.
Follow me, please.

II. Work in pairs. According to the floor plan on page 4, practise explaining the location of seats in turn with your partner with the seat numbers given in the pairwork files.

PAIRWORK	Student A Student B						
Student A randomly choose one of the numbers	B	A	D	F	E	C	K
Student B randomly choose one of the letters	33	1	29	10	17	31	12

7. Boarding announcements and safety checks.

I. Read the following announcement. Pay attention to the instructions given by flight attendants on different facilities on board, especially the verb phrases.

Good morning, ladies and gentlemen. On behalf of Captain Hopkins and the crew, I'd like to welcome you on board.

This is flight SX3692 to Hangzhou. The flight time will be about two hours and ten minutes.

We are ready for departure. Please fasten your seatbelt, open the window shade, fold your tray table, bring your seatback upright and unplug your headphones and electronic devices. Large portable electronic devices, such as laptops, should be stowed properly. Please ensure that small portable electronic devices, like cellphones, are switched to the airplane mode. Please do not smoke during the entire flight.

Thank you!

II. What to do with the circled items? Write the names of the items and use the given terms to complete the instructions you might give during a safety check.

BUZZ: How to give polite instructions? Find out what is in common with requests A to E.

PASSENGER'S PROBLEMS/REQUESTS		
fasten and tighten	fold away	switch off
stow under the seat in front of you	adjust to the upright position	

A. I'm sorry, sir/madam, but could you please *fasten your seat belt and tighten it* ?

B. Could you please _____?

C. Madam, would you please _____?

D. _____?

E. _____?

8. Listen and learn.

I. Listen to the dialogues and number the pictures in order.

II. Listen again. What did the attendant say in response to the passenger's situation in each dialogue?

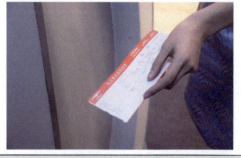

No._____
Answer_____

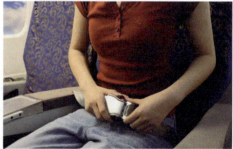

No._____
Answer_____

No._____	No._____
Answer_____	Answer_____

RESPONSE:

(1) Madam, please fasten your seat belt. We'll be taking off soon.

(2) Welcome on board, madam. May I have a look at your boarding pass, please?

(3) No, I'm afraid not, sir. Can I offer you anything else?

(4) Can I help you with this? There's more space at the back.

CLIMB

9. Explore and learn.

It is important to ask questions and give requests in a polite manner. Read the given situations and formulate your questions with the given sentence patterns.

You can ask politely using:		
Can I...	Can you please...	Would you mind...
May I...	Could you please...	Do you mind (if I)...
Should I...	Would you please...	Is it OK (for you to/if I)...

Situation 1: The flight is about to take off. You spot a passenger who hasn't had his seat belt fastened.

Situation 2: The flight is about to take off. You spot a passenger still holding his overcoat.

Situation 3: You are greeting a passenger and want to direct him to his seat.

Situation 4: The flight is about to take off. You find that a window shade has been pulled down.

Situation 5: The passengers are boarding. You find a lady trying to squeeze her hand luggage into the overhead stowage compartment.

Situation 6: The flight is about to take off. You spot a passenger still having a phone call.

Situation 7: The flight is about to take off. You see a child putting down his tray table.

Situation 8: The flight is about to take off. You spot a passenger having her seatback reclined.

10. Speak: rephrase the following sentences with the sentence patterns in the bracket.

(1) Can you fold away your tray table? (Do you mind...)
(2) Stow your bag under the seat in front of you, madam. (Would you please...)
(3) Can I help you with your luggage? (May I...)
(4) You have to adjust the seatback to the upright position. (Could you please...)
(5) Do you want to change seat with the lady over there? (Is it OK for you to...)
(6) Sir, you can't use your phone right now. (Can you please...)

11. Pronounce: listen to the recording of the following sentences and practise your pronunciation by repeating.

I. Practice the pronunciation of "could/would you".

II. Mark the different intonations with "↗" for tone up, "↘" for tone down and "∗" for stress. Practise the intonations.

III. Practise with your partner. Pay attention to the tones.
(1) Could you please remain on your seat until I've checked with the passenger list?

(2) Could you please fasten your seat belt and tighten it?

(3) Could you please adjust your seatback to the upright position?

(4) Would you please wait for a second while I go and check if we have anything left?

12. Master and practise.

I. Listen to Sarah's interview and decide if the statement is true (T), false (F) or not mentioned (NM).

(1) Ten minutes before boarding, flight attendants check the boarding music.	F
(2) Flight attendants have to check if passengers have their boarding passes.	
(3) A Boeing 747 airliner has two aisles.	
(4) There needs to be attendants in the middle of the cabin to serve food.	
(5) Passengers sometimes get annoyed when boarding.	
(6) Flight attendants need to ask passengers to sit down as quickly as possible.	
(7) For each flight, there will be different situations.	
(8) The flight attendant offers to have a look around after the plane has landed.	

II. Listen again and complete the passage below.

In this part of the interview, Sarah talked about the _____ procedures. The routine work begins with _____ the boarding music for the right volume. The music is played over the plane's loudspeaker. When the passengers begin boarding, attendants will _____ by welcoming them on board. Then they will ask the passengers to _____. To ensure that passengers can find their seats, attendants have to _____. Passengers might _____ due to various situations. So there will be cabin crew _____ to help resolve passengers' problems. But sometimes, attendants might get anxious because there are too many passengers needing help.

III. Discuss with your partner: How would you cope if the "little situations" get on your nerve during boarding? Give a brief presentation about your ways to "keep smiling".

CRUISE

13. Read and think: here's an excerpt from an interview article of two Emirates flight attendants in the TRAVEL column of Huffpost.com. Read and complete the following two tasks.

TRAVEL 11/18/2015 10:31am ET | Updated Nov 19,2015

Here's What It's ReALLY Like To Be An Emirates Flight Attendant

Flights, free housing and so much more.

Expert travelers know Emirates as one of the most luxurious airlines in the world. With opulent aircraft boasting showers, cocktail bars and sprawling first-class seats, Emirates recently welcomed a 615-seat A380 jet to its fleet, setting a record for the most passengers on a regularly-scheduled commercial flight... ever.

With aircrafts that fancy, it's no surprise that being an Emirates flight attendant looks like a pretty glamorous gig. The airline hires about 5,500 cabin crew per year, from more than 200,000 applicants who vie for a spot, according to Emirates recruitment manager Michael Gilchrist. And once they're in, the perks are beautiful: A 6-week training program and free year-round housing at headquarters in Dubai, along with travel all around the world.

We spoke with Gilchrist and Tamara White, an Emirates flight attendant of over two years, to find out what it's REALLY like to work on one of the fanciest airlines in the world.

The Huffington Post: Emirates is known as an elite airline. How does one even start the application process?

Michael Gilchrist: "You can apply online or come to an Open Day, which happens in about 50 cities globally every month. From there, we invite 50 to 200 applicants per city to Assessment Days with an info session, group exercises and an English language test."

Tamara White: "The first round on Assessment Day is a really quick, 3-minute conversation, where you're asked 'Tell me about yourself.' You also have to pass the height requirement—stand on your tiptoes to see if you can close the overhead bins."

HP: Are recruiters looking extra-closely at appearance and evaluating candidates based on their looks?

MG: "It's more about a polished, professional image than beauty. We love being able to visualize a candidate in our uniform, so it helps to show up in a well-cut suit with neat and tidy hair, simple elegant makeup, looking polished and fresh."

TW: "No, I had never been a flight attendant before. But you do need a bubbly personality."

MG: "We're looking for 'globalistas'—those people who want to travel to new and exciting cities, taste new food, experience the differences in the world. Our customers come from so many different backgrounds, and we want our crew to be open and curious about who they are. We also need to see a clear level of adaptability, because most people don't have to move overseas when they get a new job."

HP: Oh, that's right. What is it like to drop everything and move to Dubai for the job?

MG: "We have more than 60 buildings in Dubai, where our crew lives together. They build the community feel that we want—the crew is everywhere, going to the training college, or to work, or to flights. Housing is provided, which makes things easier for new crew members. They have a fully-furnished apartment ready for them."

TW: "You fly all the time, so you only have about half the month in Dubai. I have friends there, but it's hard to coordinate group outings because everyone has different travel schedules."

HP: How does travel work? Do you have a set route?

TW: "Each month you're given a roster of places. For example, next month I'm going to Toronto, Lisbon, Sydney-Auckland for a six-day trip, and Prague. Once you get your roster, you can swap with other colleagues. There's always a new destination I want to go, so I can switch."

Task 1

(1) What aspects of the flight attendant's life are covered in the interview?
(2) After reading the interview, can you tell us what you find interesting about working for Emirates?
(3) What do you think is working for Emirates different from other companies?

Task 2

Search online for articles about flight attendants' life narrated by crew members of other airline companies. Make comparisons and see if this kind of work and lifestyle is what you want. Which airline company do you aspire to go to the most?

Unit 2 Routines after Take-off

TAXI

1. Warm-up: discuss in pairs and answer the following questions.

I. What is the flight attendant in the picture doing?

II. Do you know what a safety instruction card is?

III. Complete the crossword puzzle with the given words and clues.

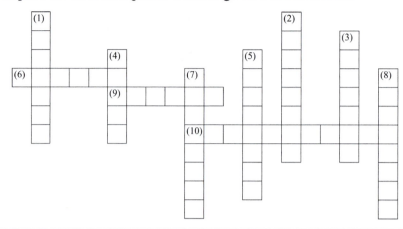

ACROSS	DOWN
(6) Make something safe.	(1) The first stage of a flight.
(9) A kind of computer that you can carry around.	(2) The part of a seat where you can lay your head.
(10) Snacks and tea.	(3) Something that keeps you warm.
	(4) Make something happen late.
	(5) The part of a cabin seat for your feet.
	(7) Getting on the plane.
	(8) Something that keeps you safe on seat.

blanket   seat belt   laptop   headrest   boarding
secure   delay   take-off   footrest   refreshment

2. Spot: categorize the passengers in the pictures with the given tags.

A. a mother with children   B. a nervous first-time passenger
C. a big family   D. a pregnant woman
E. an ill woman   F. an elderly couple

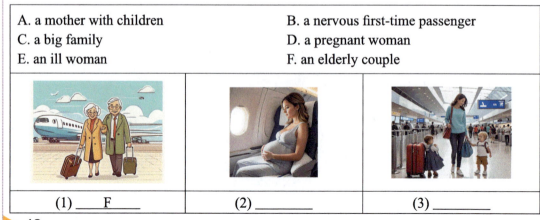

(1) ___F___   (2) _____   (3) _____

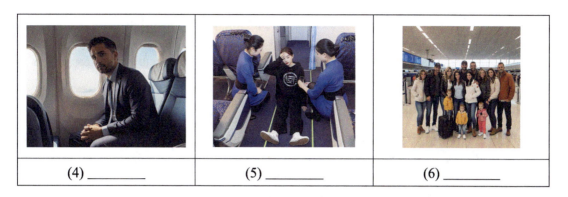

| (4) _____ | (5) _____ | (6) _____ |

3. **Brainstorm: what other types of passengers will you meet on board?**

e.g. a young man with a guitar

4. **Converse: work with a partner. Choose one of the passengers from the list in task 3 and try offering help with the following given sentence patterns.**

Identify problem: Sir/Madam, how can I help/everything all right?
Respond: Let's see/I see/Don't worry.
Offer: I'll...in just a second.

TAKE-OFF

5. **Complete the conversations with the words below. Pay attention to how the flight attendants solved the passagers' problems.**

air-conditioner	heated	knob
spare	repeated	connection

Conversation (1)
Flight attendant A: Oh my god! I've _____ many times and look, there are

passengers moving around the cabin.

Flight attendant B: Don't worry. Let's get the meals _____ and the trolley out. I will ask the passengers to watch out for the trolley.

Conversation (2)
Passenger: Excuse me, miss. It's terribly hot now. How can I use the _____?
Flight attendant: You may start the air conditioner by turning this ___ to the right.

Conversation (3)
Passenger: Excuse me, miss. Could you _____ me some time?
Flight attendant: Sure.
Passenger: Is the flight going to arrive at Shanghai on schedule?
Flight attendant: Yes, I think so.
Passenger: That's good. I'm worried because I have a very tight _____. Thank you.
Flight attendant: It's my pleasure.

CLIMB

6. Explore and learn: match the request during take-off with passenger's response.

Request	Response
A. Excuse me, sir. Could you keep your son's feet off the seat in front?	① No problem. Can you tell me how to adjust the seatback again?
B. Would it be possible to adjust your seat back to the upright position, sir?	② Oh, I'm really sorry. John, put down your legs.
C. Would you mind putting your footrest up now?	③ Why? The sun is in my eyes!
D. Could you possibly open your window shade for take-off?	④ Oh, all right.
E. Do you think you could put your bag under the seat in front of you?	⑤ Do I have to? Where should I put my feet then?
F. I'm sorry, but could you please fold up your tray table?	⑥ Sure. I will put it up.

7. Language focus: describing problems.

I. We use past participles as adjectives or nouns to describe problems. Study these sentences.

With past participles as adjectives	With nouns
The screen is broken.	It has spots on the screen.
The armrests are stained.	They have a stain on them.
The tray table surface is damaged.	There is some damage on the surface.

II. Read the comments from passengers on a flight. Write sentences in two different ways using forms of the word in parentheses. Then compare with a partner.

(1) The air-conditioner doesn't work well. It... (break)
_____
_____

(2) The cushion on the seat looks pretty dirty. It... (stain)
_____
_____

(3) Could you bring me another cup of tea? This plastic cup...(chip)
_____
_____

(4) The flight attendant needs a new uniform. The one she is wearing...(tear)
_____
_____

III. Group work: look around your classroom. How many problems can you identify?

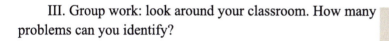

e.g. The window is cracked.
(1) _____.
(2) _____.
(3) _____.
(4) _____.
(5) _____.
(6) _____.

8. Pronunciation: linked sounds.

I. Listen and repeat the sentences. Final consonant sounds are often linked to the vowel sounds that follow them.

(1) Excuse me, I think there's‿a problem with this headrest.
(2) Would‿it be OK for me to upgrade to business class?
(3) Would you turn‿off your power bank?
(4) Could you please put‿it‿in the overhead compartment or stow‿it under the seat‿in front‿of you?

II. Mark the linked sounds in the sentences below. Listen and check. Then practise reading the sentences.

(1) I'm afraid that I don't understand English.

(2) The temperature in the cabin will drop as soon as the plane stops climbing.

(3) Give a brief introduction of the weather conditions at the destination.

(4) Let me get a wet towel for you.

III. Practise with your partner. Pay attention to the linked sounds.

9. Converse: work with a partner. Take turns to practise responding and offering help under the following two situations.

Situation I: A passenger was feeling cold and pressed the call button during take-off. You should come to the passenger and solve this problem.

Situation II: A lady pressed the call button as she wanted to know the flight time and wondered if she could have meal early. Come and help the lady.

10. Brainstorm: what points should cabin crew bear in mind during take-off?

Points
e.g. Panic Control

11. Master and practise.

I. Listen to the captain's announcement and complete the announcement during take-off.

Ladies and gentlemen, this is your captain speaking. We have left Shanghai for Osaka. The_____is 1,350 kilometers and it takes about two hours. The cruising altitude is 9,500 meters. We are_____to arrive at Kansai International Airport at about 14:00 (local time). The weather today is very good, and I wish you all a pleasant journey with_____. Thank you.

II. Listen to the purser giving further information to the passengers and complete the announcement.

Ladies and Gentlemen, it's great to have you on board. In_____with CAAC regulations, _____is not allowed during the whole flight. There is a lunch service on today's flight. You can use the in-flight_____system throughout the flight. Duty free items are_____for purchase shortly after the lunch. Please refer to the shopping on board magazine in the seat pocket in front of you.

Please remain seated and keep your seat belt fastened in case of sudden turbulence. If there is anything we can do for you, please press the_____and we will come to you right after.

We'll begin our_____service in about 15 minutes. This is a short flight, so please kindly look at the menu card in your seat pocket and have your orders ready. As the_____ pass through the cabin, please keep the aisles clear. Thank you.

III. Listen again to parts of the announcement and practise the sentences.
(1) Ladies and gentlemen, it's great to have you on board. In accordance with CAAC regulations, smoking is not allowed during the whole flight.
(2) Duty free items are available for purchase shortly after the lunch. Please refer to the

shopping on board magazine in the seat pocket in front of you.

(3) Please remain seated and keep your seat belt fastened in case of sudden turbulence.

IV. Work with a partner and practise making the second announcement. First read it aloud then try to make the announcement without the script.

CRUISE

12. Read and think: read the following passage and complete the tasks.

Best Ways to Tackle Cabin Crew Tiredness

For those working as cabin crew, tiredness, unfortunately, comes with the job. If you're feeling tired all the time—at work, at home, on a night out, then you're probably finding it pretty frustrating.

There are ways to help reduce fatigue once you can establish the cause, so first of all have a think about your lifestyle and how that could be affecting your energy level. The more you do to improve your physical well-being generally, the better your body will cope with flying across time zones and working irregular hours. So begin by assessing your physical and emotional states—if these are out of order, your tiredness level may soar while working as cabin crew.

Weight issues

Being overweight or underweight are the two most common causes for feeling tired all the time. If you are overweight your body has to work harder and if you are under-weighted, your body doesn't have enough energy to burn and it has to work overtime to keep you going.

Irregular sleep patterns

If you are suffering from insomnia—not able to get to sleep or waking up at irregular times—there are many options open to you. You might want to invest in special light box and find out about the benefits of Light Therapy. You can also learn relaxation techniques or self-hypnosis which will help you get off to sleep. And there are many natural sleeping tablets to consider. Of course consult your doctor if you are unsure of how to progress.

Emotional state causes tiredness.

If you work antisocial hours or irregular shifts this could be a contributing factor to the fatigue you feel every day. Of course, you can't just up and change your career at the drop of a hat; so what can you do about it?

If you find yourself feeling regularly bored, anxious, resentful, worried or panicked you are more than likely experiencing feelings of tiredness as well. One thing that you can do to help control your tiredness is to actually take up an activity—we're not talking running marathons here, but a twice-weekly exercise or dance class can relieve stress and boredom and promote the release of the happy hormone serotonin which will make you feel more awake and more fulfilled.

Overcoming Jet Lag

According to medical specialists Bupa, there aren't any medicines specifically available for jet lag. However, there's evidence to suggest that the hormone melatonin can be useful in people who are travelling across more than five time zones. Melatonin has not been licensed yet for jet lag, but if a doctor who specializes in travel has experience in this area, he or she may be able to prescribe it to you as an off-license medication. Talk to a doctor at a travel clinic if you're travelling somewhere where you think you will need this treatment.

If you're tired when you need to be alert, caffeine can help as a temporary pick-up. But don't drink lots of coffee in the hours before you need to get to sleep.

Think positively about your job

The other thing you can do is to tackle the bits and pieces in your life that you feel may be responsible for your tiredness; if your job is one which you don't want to leave but you're not all that happy with it either, then try and find the positives in it—you're progressing in your career, albeit a little slowly, and you're socializing everyday with people from all walks of life. It's a fantastic job, if you can see beyond the tiredness!

Task 1

According to the passage, what can you do to reduce cabin crew tiredness?

(1) __e.g. *maintain regular sleep time*.__
(2) _____
(3) _____
(4) _____
(5) _____

Task 2

Decide if the statement is true (T), false (F) or not mentioned (NM).

(1) Cabin crew feel tired both at work and at home.	
(2) Being overweight or underweight is not the reason for fatigue.	
(3) Sleeping less than seven hours during the night can cause tiredness.	
(4) Taking up an activity can control your tiredness.	
(5) Caffeine can solve the jet lag problem completely.	

Unit 3 Passenger Comfort

TAXI

1. Warm-up: discuss in pairs and answer the following questions.

I. What is the situation with the two passengers in the picture?

II. Have you ever been in a similar situation? How did you deal with it?

III. Complete the crossword puzzle with the given words and clues.

ACROSS	DOWN
(2) Let something fall down. (4) Trouble. (6) People who take the plane. (7) Get to a place. (8) Rubbish. (9) You feel_____when you lie on your bed.	(1) You put your bags in the_____ over your head. (3) Ask for something. (5) You pack your things in your_____ when traveling. (9) You_____ when you are really sad.

arrival   cry   request   baggage   problem
passenger   comfortable   drop   waste   compartment

2. **Spot**: what is the problem the passenger(s) in each picture is/are having?

A. a question about the time of arrival
B. a cold passenger
C. a request for a waste bag
D. a dropped phone
E. a request to open the baggage compartment
F. a crying baby

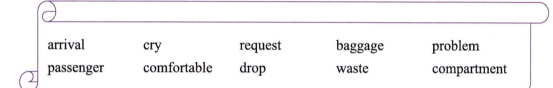

(1) __F__   (2) _____   (3) _____

(4) _____   (5) _____   (6) _____

3. Brainstorm: what other situations you may encounter when making sure passengers' comfort on board?

e.g. *a seat with broken seatback*

4. Converse: choose one of the passengers from the list in task 3 and try offering help with the following given sentence patterns.

Identify problem: Sir/Madam, how can I help/everything all right?
Respond: Let's see/I see/Don't worry.
Offer: I'll...in just a second.

TAKE-OFF

5. Understand passengers' requests.

I. What are the circled facilities in the picture? What problems/requests will the passengers have with these items?

22

Passenger's Problems/Requests		
fix	put down/back	open/close
switch on/off	turn up/down	recline/adjust

E.g. A passenger might ask the flight attendant to *fix the armrest* .

(1) _____.
(2) _____.
(3) _____.
(4) _____.
(5) _____.
(6) _____.

II. Why are the passengers in Picture 1 uncomfortable? What amenities do they need from Picture 2? Match the passenger names with their problems and the amenities they need.

Picture 1

Picture 2

Passenger's Problems/Requests		
Joey	thirsty	blanket
Ross	hungry	newspaper
Phoebe	cold	waste bag
Monica	bored	snack
Chandler	nauseous	drink

BUZZ I: What should the flight attendant say when a passenger needs help?

BUZZ II: How could you express possibility?

E.g. (1) Joey might be <u>nauseous</u>. She might ask for <u>a waste bag</u>.
  (2) _____.
  (3) _____.
  (4) _____.
  (5) _____.

6. Listen and learn. 🔊

BUZZ III: How did the flight attendants respond to the requests? How did they offer help?

I. Listen to the dialogues and number the pictures in order.

II. Listen again. How did the flight attendant reply to passengers' needs? Match the answers with the corresponding pictures.

No._____ Answer_____	No._____ Answer_____
No._____ Answer_____	No._____ Answer_____

民航乘务英语

Answer:

(1) Don't worry, sir. I'll be back with your bag in just a second.

(2) Let's see. We'll be arriving at our destination in about an hour, sir.

(3) I see, madam… I'll go and check if I can find anything to calm him down.

(4) I'm sorry but I can bring you a blanket instead. Does that sound okay to you, sir?

CLIMB

7. Explore and learn: what kind of help would be offered following each response? Match the request with the corresponding response and offer.

Request	Response + Offer
A. Can I have some water, please?	(1) Not at all. Still got one sanitary bag here.
B. Could you ask the lady to stop talking so loudly?	(2) Certainly/Not a problem. I'll get you water right now, sir.
C. Can I have today's *People's Daily*, please?	(3) I'm sorry. You really have to let your kid go back to his seat. It's too dangerous.
D. Do you mind bringing me a sanitary bag?	(4) Let's see/Let me check. I'll be back with your bag in just a second.
E. Can you help fetch my bag, please?	(5) I'm sorry. I'll go and talk to the lady.
F. Can I carry my baby?	(6) I'm afraid not. We don't have *People's Daily*. Will *China Daily* be okay for you?

8. Write: Fill in the blanks with appropriate responses and offers.

(1)
Passenger: Could you please bring me another headphone, please? This one is not working.

Flight attendant: (Response) _____. I'll get you a headphone in just a second.

(2)
Passenger: Excuse me. Are there many people queuing for the lavatory right now?
Flight attendant: (Response)_____. No, sir. There's no one queuing right now.

(3)
Passenger: Excuse me. Do you happen to have kiwi juice?
Flight attendant: (Response) _____. But we do have apple juice and orange juice if you want.

(4)
Passenger: Hi there. The kid behind me keeps kicking my backrest. It's annoying.
Flight attendant: (Response) _____. I'll go and talk to the mother.

(5)
Passenger: Sorry. I can't unbuckle my seat belt. Can you help?
Flight attendant: (Response) _____. (Offer)_____
_____.

(6)
Passenger: Hi miss. I'm bored here. Can you play something fun on the TV?
Flight attendant: (Response) _____. (Offer)_____
_____.

9. **Pronounce: listen to the recording of the following answers and practise your pronunciation by repeating after.** 🔊

I. Practise the pronunciation of "**ll**".

II. Mark the different intonations with "↗" for tone up, "↘" for tone down and "＊" for stress. Practise the intonations.

III. Practise with your partner. Pay attention to the tones.

(1) Don't worry, sir. It'll be fine.

(2) I see, madam. I'll go and check if I can find anything to calm him down.

(3) Let's see. We'll be arriving at our destination in about an hour, sir.

(4) Certainly, madam. That'll be my pleasure.

(5) I'm afraid not, sir. You'll have to fasten your seat belt now.

(6) I'm sorry, but I can bring you a blanket instead. Will that do for you, sir?

10. Converse: work with a partner. Take turns to practise responding and offering help under the following two situations.

Situation 1: It was about to begin initial descent. Gary in 36B dropped his phone under the seat in front of him and could not find it. He asked for help finding the phone.

Situation 2: It was during the cruise. Sharon in 9A was eating the snacks she brought on board. Her sanitary bag was full so she asked for an extra sanitary bag.

11. Brainstorm: what kind of requests should be satisfied and what should not? Try to give a list of the "YES" requests and "NO" requests.

"YES" Requests	"NO" Requests
e.g. *asking for some water*	e.g. *asking for personal information*

12. Master and practise.

I. Listen to the conversation and decide if the statement is true (T) or false (F).

(1) The first passenger did not buckle his seat belt.	T
(2) The first passenger was sick because he was cold.	
(3) The flight attendant offered to get some water and a towel.	
(4) The first passenger was annoyed by the crying baby.	
(5) The baby was crying because she lost her Barbie doll.	
(6) The flight attendant finally found the toy that the baby lost.	
(7) The flight attendant borrowed a teddy bear from another passenger.	
(8) The flight attendant offered to have a look around after the plane landed.	

II. Listen again and complete the passage below.

The flight attendant asked the passenger to ____(1)____ . But she found out that the passenger ____(2)____ . The flight attendant asked the lady to ____(3)____ and offered to ____(4)____ . She instructed the lady to ____(5)____ . The passenger then made a complaint about ____(6)____ . So the flight attendant offered to ____(7)____ .

The flight attendant went to talk to the mother. She was told that the baby was crying because ____(8)____ . The flight attendant offered to ____(9)____ and came back with ____(10)____ . She also offered to ____(11)____ after the plane landed. The mother expressed her gratitude.

III. Discuss with your partner: what would you do if the baby won't stop crying? Demonstrate with a role-play skit.

CRUISE

13. Read and think: read the following passage and complete the two tasks.

THREE Qualities Cabin Crew Recruiters Look For

Empathy

Empathy isn't just for passengers but co-workers too. On the day of the interview, show kindness to the other applicants. Smile. Talk. Help. Give way to other applicants. Don't ever try to put someone else down just so you could shine.

Be humane. Be genuine.

Customer Service Orientation

You'll be asked a lot of problem-solving questions. Whenever you answer one, always keep the customer your top priority. You might be asked to talk about:
- *a situation when you have delivered excellent service*
- *how you handle a difficult customer*
- *an experience of resolving a customer complaint successfully*
- *whether you think customer is always right*

These questions bring out how good you are at solving passenger problems—leaving them feeling satisfied, appreciated, and heard. In your answers, show that you have the customers' best interests in mind. Offer alternatives rather than only one solution. Let the customers choose the solution they desire.

Adaptability

Your plans to spend a weekend with loved ones could be cancelled due to schedule changes. You'll have standby duties and may have to be ready for duty within 20 minutes of being called. You're definitely going to experience flight delays and cancellations.

You may expect to have 30 minutes to do your pre-flight ground duties but now you only have five minutes. You may not have all the resources you have expected to perform a job correctly. But you'll have to be able to make it happen. Your company's policies could change overnight.

All these sudden changes do happen very often and recruiters want to see how well you can cope with disruptions. You might be asked to describe:
- *a big change you've had to deal with*
- *a time when you had to improvise to achieve your goal*

In your answer, tell a story where you welcomed the change. Mention the positive results from it. End by talking about what you've learned from the experience.

Keep these qualities glued to the back of your head throughout your entire interview. Whatever you say or do, always tailor your words and actions to these qualities.

"Show that you think of change as an opportunity to grow, not an ordeal to endure."

—— James Reed

Task 1

(1) What are the three qualities that the recruiters are looking for? Try to explain in your own words.

(2) Why are the recruiters looking for these three qualities?

(3) Which one do you think is the most important quality and which one is the least important? Why?

Task 2

You are preparing for an interview for Air China. How would you show the recruiters that you have the three qualities?

Unit 4 Food and Dirnks Service

TAXI

1. Warm-up: discuss in pairs and answer the following questions.

I. What is the flight attendant doing in the picture?

II. How do you like the in-flight meals?

III. Complete the crossword puzzle with the given words and clues.

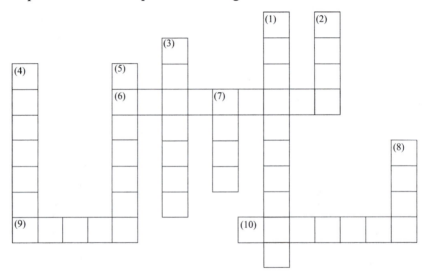

ACROSS	DOWN
(6) Explain why somebody should choose the item. (9) Hot. (10) The cabin kitchen.	(1) Generally used to refer to someone who doesn't eat meat. (2) Not strong. (3) Beer or wine. (4) We offer passengers with different meal_____. (5) Cabin crew store meals in the_____. (7) Sir, please have a look at today's. (8) Where you can put your meal.

| alcohol | galley | recommend | spicy | mild |
| choices | menu | trolley | tray | vegetarian |

2. Spot: match the food with the pictures.

A. soft drink   B. steak
C. brownie   D. salad
E. alcohol   F. butter and roll

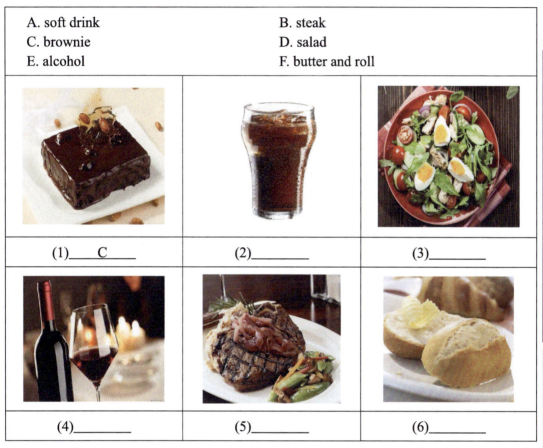

(1) ___C___   (2) _____   (3) _____

(4) _____   (5) _____   (6) _____

Unit 4 Food and Drinks Service

3. Brainstorm: what other food might be served on board?

(1) e.g. *yogurt* _____   (4) _____
(2) _____   (5) _____
(3) _____   (6) _____

4. Converse: work with a partner and talk about your favorite food. You should specify: the type and the taste of this food that you like and why you like it.

TAKE-OFF

5. Food on the meal tray.

I. Listen and label the objects on the meal tray.

(1) ___dessert/ice-cream___
(2) _____
(3) _____
(4) _____
(5) _____
(6) _____
(7) _____
(8) _____
(9) _____
(10) _____

II. Listen again and complete the sentences.

(1) _____ a little spicy.
(2) _____ cooked with broccoli and cheese.
(3) There is also a roll with _____ butter.
(4) It's _____ with ice-cream.
(5) Do you _____ brown sugar or white sugar?
(6) It's a _____ of vegetables.

III. Read and study the sentence patterns.

Sentence patterns for describing food
It's a little spicy.
It's served with French fries.
It's cooked with (spinach).
It's a kind of fish/vegetable.
There's also a box of ice cream.
It's steamed/grilled/roasted/fried/boiled.
It's served cold/hot.

IV. Work with a partner and practise describing the meal in the picture to the passengers with the sentence patterns above.

6. Serving drinks.

I. Which categories do the listed beverages belong to? Tick the category that matches the given drink.

Drink Menu	Alcohol	Soft Drinks	Hot Drinks
vodka	√		
Earl Grey tea			
whisky			
coffee			
rum			
coke			
espresso			
champagne			
lemonade			
sparkling water			
Seven Up			
Fanta			
fruit juice			
Sprite			
red wine			
peppermint tea			
white wine			

Drink Menu	Alcohol	Soft Drinks	Hot Drinks
cocktail			
hot chocolate			
beer			
Martini			
black tea			
gin and tonic			
green tea			

II. Can you think of other kinds of drinks other than the listed ones?

(1) _mocha_
(2) _____
(3) _____
(4) _____
(5) _____
(6) _____

7. Listen and learn.

I. Listen to the conversations. What does each passenger order and do they get what they want?

Passenger	Main course	Drinks	What they get
(1)	roasted chicken		
(2)			
(3)			

II. Listen again and complete the phrases of offering and ordering food.

Offering food	Making orders
(1) Would you like something to_____? (2) How about _____? (3) May I_____a drink, madam? (4) What would you like to_____for lunch, sir?	(1) Do you have_____? (2) Could I have_____? (3) Whisky_____, please. (4) Black tea with_____, please.
Apologizing	Giving the meal tray
(1) I'm sorry for_____you waiting. (2) I'm_____that we've run out of the cheeseburger. (3) I do_____.	(1) There you_____, madam. (2) Here you_____, sir.

III. Listen and read the sentences in task II. Pay attention to the intonation pattern.

IV. Practise providing meal service and ordering food with a partner.

CLIMB

8. Explore and learn: direct and reported statements.

Direct statements		Reported statements
I'd like a glass of water.	She said (that)	She'd like a glass of water.
I can't have spicy food.		She couldn't have spicy food.
I would like to have a vegetarian meal.	The passenger told me (that)	She would like to have a vegetarian meal.
I'd like my whisky on the rocks.		He'd like his whisky on the rocks.

Imagine you are a passenger and the person next to you doesn't understand English. Work with a partner and help the passenger to order food using reported statements.

9. **Making an apology.**

Complete the conversation between a flight attendant and a passenger during the meals service.

turbulence	coffee	green tea	mind	another
selection	pain	terribly	sorry	apologize

Flight attendant: Hello, madam, we have a_____of soft drinks, alcohol and hot drinks. What would you like to drink?
Passenger: What kind of tea do you have?
Flight attendant: We have Earl Grey, _____, oolong and peppermint tea.
Passenger: Do you have jasmine tea?
Flight attendant: I'm _____, madam. I'm afraid we don't have jasmine tea on board today. Would you like something else?
Passenger: I'd like a cup of_____with sugar.
Flight attendant: Sure. Here is your coffee. Be careful. It's quite hot.
(At the moment, the plane was encountering some_____.)
Passenger: Ouch!
Flight attendant: I'm_____sorry about it! I'll clean it for you in a second. Are you all right? Do you feel any_____?
Passenger: Never_____. It's not your fault.
Flight attendant: I do_____for that. Thank you for your understanding.
Passenger: That's all right.
Flight attendant: I'll get you_____cup of coffee.
Passenger: OK.

10. **Pronounce: Intonation in questions of choice.**

I. Listen and repeat the questions. Notice how the intonation changes at the end.
(1) Would you like to have mocha or cappuccino?
(2) Would you like your whisky straight or on the rocks?
(3) How do you like your tea, weak or strong?
(4) We have a selection of soft drinks. Do you want Coke, Fanta or Sprite?
(5) How do you like your steak, rare, medium or well done?
(6) Green tea or black tea?

II. Mark the six sentences above with the different intonations("↗" for tone up, "↘" for tone down and "*" for stress). Practise the intonations.

11. Master and practise.

I. Listen and try to complete the announcement before meal service.

Ladies and gentlemen, the_____sign has been switched off and you can move around the_____. Our in-flight meal service will begin shortly so please_____for the trolley. Please_____the tray table in front of you. We have three_____for the main course which are beef with potatoes, fish with rice and_____lasagna. Today's_____is chocolate brownie. We offer a selection of_____and cold beverages including coffee, tea and soft drinks. Alcohol like wine, beer and cocktail are also_____on board.

Please check the menu card in your seat_____and have your order ready. Thank you and enjoy your flight.

II. Choose the best word or phrase to complete each sentence.
(1) The seatbelt sign has been switched off means (   )
A. You should fasten your seatbelt immediately.
B. You can feel free to walk around the cabin.
C. The seatbelt sign has been on.

(2) Our in-flight meal service will begin shortly means (　)

A. The meal service will not begin.

B. The meal service will soon begin.

C. The meal service has already begun.

(3) We offer a selection of complimentary drinks means they are (　)

A. expensive.

B. free of charge.

C. served in business class only.

(4) Beer, cocktail and wine contain (　)

A. milk.　　　　　B. caffeine.　　　　　C. alcohol.

(5) Watch out for the trolley means (　)

A. take care of the trolley.

B. don't block the trolley.

C. be ready with your order.

III. Work with a partner and practise making the announcement. First read it aloud, then try to remember it and say it from memory.

CRUISE

12. Read and think: read the following passage and complete the tasks.

What You Never Knew About Your In-flight Meal

We all like to complain about airline food, but there is a tremendous amount of effort that goes into keeping us fed at 35,000 feet. And the things airlines and their caterers need to worry about are things that would never, ever occur to us while we're mindlessly tucking into our in-flight meals.

Cans of Coke, for example—there's a reason why it's so much more expensive on planes. Or why ice-cream is such a problem. Or why passengers say they want to see healthy food on the menu but opt for the naughty option almost every single time.

Ice cream on planes is a big problem.

It's the tasty treat we're lucky to score with our in-flight dinner but ice-cream, like other dairy products, is a huge challenge for airlines and caterers, Ms De Hauw said.

"Ice cream that is supplied but not consumed is wasted,"she said.

"Everything that is milk-based is difficult too（because of temperature reasons）."

Ms De Hauw said raw fish was also difficult to serve on flights. "It needs to be extremely fresh to be good," she said. "And the supply chain for airline catering is not tailored for very fresh foods."

> "People have no idea of the complexity behind airline meals—the safety standards, the supply chains, the number of meals we have to prepare for each flight."
>
> ——Anne De Hauw, Gate Group

People always order the comfort food.

Ms De Hauw said while customers said they wanted to see healthy food on the in-flight menu, it was rarely what they ordered off the menu. She said one of Gate Group's airline clients boarded planes with a single fruit salad, which often, no one would ask for.

"Passengers like to see a healthy option but they're not buying it," Ms De Hauw said.

She said people typically opted for the "guilty pleasure" food.

"We have done research and actually people, unconsciously, look to comfort themselves because there's that sentiment of fear and uncertainty," she said.

"And they're also not that comfortable on the flight, because they're sitting in a seat with everybody on top of each other. People are looking to pass time, and food is one way to do that. We usually allow more guilty pleasures in the air than on the ground."

Airline food is some of the safest you can eat.

Ms De Hauw's company, Gate Group, made headlines this month when the harmful bacteria listeria was found in its drains and on the ground of its unit at Los Angeles International Airport, prompting a number of its high-profile clients from the company. She said the company immediately took action to have the bacteria removed and is reconstructing its LA base. Ms De Hauw added that airline food was among the safest in the world.

"It takes on average about 24 hours between the food production and the moment that the passenger eats the food," she said.

"An airline cannot have their passengers become sick from their meals. It's a very safe food experience, that's for sure."

Task 1

According to the passage, what do you know about in-flight meals?

Task 2

Decide if the statement is true (T), false (F) or not mentioned (NM).

(1) In-flight meals are never tasty.	
(2) Everything that is milk-based needs to be fresh.	
(3) Food is a good way to pass time.	
(4) People tend to eat healthier when they are on board.	
(5) Airline food is the safest food according to the author.	

Unit 5　Health and Medical Issues

TAXI

1. Warm-up: discuss in pairs and answer the following questions.

I. What is the situation in the picture?

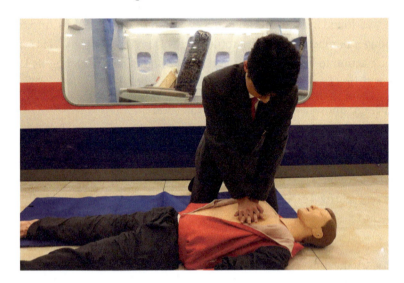

II. Have you ever been in or witnessed a similar situation? What did you do then?

III. Name the parts of the body with words from the box. Complete the crossword puzzle with the given words and clues.

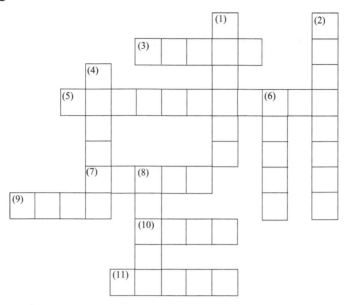

ACROSS	DOWN
(3) I injured my _____ when playing basketball yesterday. (5) Pain in the stomach. (7) If you have a _____ in the leg, your leg cannot move. (9) A giraffe have a long_____. (10) I played football with my colleague yesterday and injured my right_____. (11) High body temperature.	(1) Difficulty of breathing. (2) I accidentally cut myself and now I'm _____. (4) Heart _____ often happens to the elderlies. (6) She crossed her arms in front of her _____. (8) The part connecting your feet and legs.

fever	neck	bleeding	asthma	chest	wrist
stomachache	ankle	heart attack	cramp	stomach	knee

2. Spot: what might be the issue with the passenger in each picture?

A. fever	B. heart attack
C. asthma	D. nose bleeding
E. stomachache	F. cramp

43

(1) __E__ (2) _____ (3) _____

(4) _____ (5) _____ (6) _____

3. Brainstorm: what other health and medical issues the passengers might have on board? Use the sentence pattern of the given example.

e.g. Passengers **might suffer from** *headache*.

4. Converse: work with a partner. Choose one of the health and medical issues from the list and try offering help.

TAKE-OFF

5. Identify passengers' conditions.

I. What is the passenger's condition? Match his/her description to the corresponding conditions in the answer box and choose the right remedy for the passenger.

	Condition	Remedy		Condition	Remedy
John		①	Jane		
David			Alexander		
Alice			April		

Answer Box	
heart attack	cold
food poisoning	spasm
asthma	injury

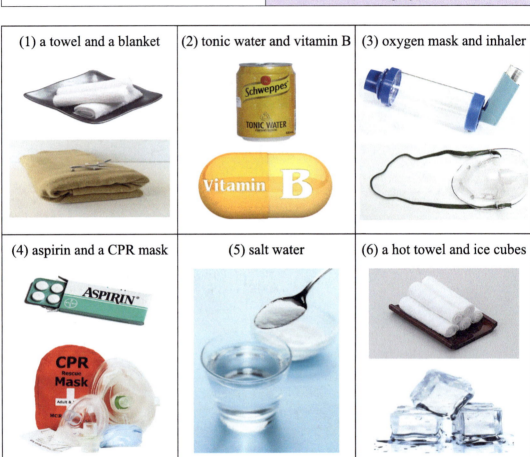

(1) a towel and a blanket
(2) tonic water and vitamin B
(3) oxygen mask and inhaler
(4) aspirin and a CPR mask
(5) salt water
(6) a hot towel and ice cubes

II. Complete the sentences according to the given example.
E.g.

Conversation (1)
Flight Attendant: Sir, *are you all right*?
John: My throat is sore… I feel really cold. And I've been shivering for quite a while.
Flight Attendant: *I think you might* be having a fever. *I'll get you* a towel and a blanket. *I would suggest* that you keep yourself warm.

Conversation (2)
Flight Attendant: Sir, _____?

David: My left calf… I cannot move my leg. It hurts really bad. Oh my goodness.
Flight Attendant: I think you might be having_____. I'll get you_____. *I would suggest that* you try to stretch your leg as much as you can.

Conversation (3)
Flight Attendant: _____?
Alice: My daughter… She cannot breathe. She's been wheezing. Please help her!
Flight Attendant: Yes, madam. I'll_____. You must help her take deep breaths.

Conversation (4)
Flight Attendant: _____?
Jane: Please help my husband! He's about to faint. The chest pain is killing him!
Flight Attendant: I'll_____immediately. You must help him take deep breaths.

Conversation (5)
Flight Attendant: _____?
Alexander: Oh it hurts… My stomach. Must be the salmon I ate.
Flight Attendant: I'll_____immediately. I would suggest that_____.

Conversation (6)
Flight Attendant: _____?
April: Sorry. I must look terrible. I don't feel anything really…except for a slight dizziness. Didn't realize it until my husband handed me the tissue.
Flight Attendant: Don't worry, madam I'll_____ immediately. Meanwhile, I would suggest that_____ _____.

BUZZ: When should the flight attendant use "suggest" and when to use "must/should/have to"?

6. Listen and learn. 🔊

I. Listen to the dialogues and number the pictures in order.
II. Listen again. How did the flight attendant reply to passengers' conditions? Match the answers with the corresponding pictures.

No._____	No._____
Answer_____	Answer_____

Unit 5　Health and Medical Issues

47

No._____	No._____
Answer_____	Answer_____

REPLY:
(1) I would suggest you drink more hot water and keep yourself warm.
(2) We have to perform a CPR immediately.
(3) You must not touch the injured area with bare hand.
(4) I would suggest that you don't take in any solid food for the next hour or so.

CLIMB

7. Explore and learn: when to use "suggest" and when to use "must/should/have to"? Choose the one you think that fits into the context.

Conversation (1)
P: Oh god. The headache is killing me.
C: _____ you take a nap.

Conversation (2)
P: Can you get me some hot water, please? I think I've got a cold.
C: No problem, sir. _____ you keep yourself warm.

Conversation (3)
P: I can't feel my left arm. Please! I'm gonna die!
C: Madam. _____ stay calm. We've got crew member professionally trained to help you relief the pain.

Conversation (4)
P: We need help. Please. My husband is unconscious.
C: Madam. _____ as my colleague to perform a CPR. Please if you could help us take off his top as quickly as possible

Conversation (5)
P: Ah! No. No. No…Don't touch it! It hurts!
C: I'm so sorry, sir. But I'll have to disinfect the wounded area. _____ endure the pain and try to stay still. It'll be really quick.

8. Write: fill in the blanks with appropriate responses and offers.

Situation I
Passenger: My stomach is not well. I feel a bit sick and heartburn. I think it's indigestion.
Flight Attendant: _____some anti-indigestion pills and hot water. _____stand up and have a walk for a few minutes. It's good for your digestive system.

Situation II
Passenger: The itchiness started right after I had that salad. I think it's the sesame in it. I'm allergic to sesames.
Flight Attendant: _____some antihistamines. _____scratch the itchy spots.

Situation III
Passenger: My chest feels tight. And I cannot breathe properly.
Flight Attendant: _____an oxygen mask. _____.

Situation IV
Passenger: I'm gonna throw up. The nausea is killing me.
Flight Attendant: _____. My colleague and I will help you move to the makeshift emergency bunk.

9. Pronounce: Listen to the recording of the following answers and practise your pronunciation by repeating 🔊

I. Practise the pronunciation of "**get you**".

II. Mark the different intonations with "↗" for tone up, "↘" for tone down and "*" for stress. Practise the intonations.

III. Practise with your partner. Pay attention to the tones.
(1) I'll get you a towel and a blanket. I would suggest that you keep yourself warm.

(2) I'll get you some anti-indigestion pills and hot water.

(3) I'll get you antiseptic wipes for disinfection.

(4) Don't panic, madam. We've got crew member professionally trained to deal with this kind of emergencies.

(5) Please stay calm, sir.

(6) I would suggest that you don't take in any solid food for an hour or so.

10. Converse: work with a partner. Take turns to practise coping with the following medical emergencies.

Situation I: It was during the cruise. Rebecca in 38B reported having dizziness and chest tightness.

Situation II: It was during the cruise. Michael in 19E reported food poisoning, diarrhea and dehydration.

11. Brainstorm: what kind of medical emergencies would require further steps than flight attendants' assistance? Try to think of examples of such grave situations.

Medical emergencies	
e.g. a woman about to labor	

12. Master and practise.

I. Listen to the conversation and decide if the statement is true (T), false (F) or not mentioned (NM).

(1) The man felt dizzy because he bumped his head.	F
(2) The man had a phobia about blood.	
(3) The cut was not that severe but the man had lost blood.	
(4) The flight attendant offered to get antiseptic wipes.	
(5) The flight attendant asked the man not to look at his wound.	
(6) The man fainted at the sight of the wound.	
(7) The flight attendant asked another passenger to operate a CPR.	
(8) The passengers sitting next to the man had to empty their seats for the CPR.	

II. Listen again and complete the passage below.

The passenger accidentally cut his leg and reported to feel __(1)__. He had blood phobia and is __(2)__. The flight attendant offered to __(3)__, but when she came back, the man __(4)__. So the flight attendant asked one of her colleagues for __(5)__. The passenger sitting next to the man, who was __(6)__ offered to __(7)__.

CRUISE

13. Read and think: read the following passage and complete the two tasks.

Medical Personnel for Air Medical Services

Historically, the need for a Physician/Nurse combination has diminished with more protocol and evidence-based applications for care by nurses and other clinicians and so the inclusion of respiratory therapists in all modes of air transport is becoming more prominent.

Retrieval Doctor/Physician

Criteria for working as a medical doctor in aeromedical services depend on the jurisdiction. In Australia, where aeromedical retrieval medicine is a well-established medical field, retrieval doctors must be experienced in a critical care specialty as fully qualified specialists, specialty registrars in advanced stages of training, or general practitioners with broad experience in critical care and obstetrics.

Flight Paramedic

A flight paramedic is a licensed paramedic with additional training as a certified flight paramedic (FP-C). The flight paramedic is usually highly trained with at least five years of autonomous clinical experience in high acuity environments of both pre-hospital emergency medicine and critical care transport. Flight paramedics may be certified as a FP-C or a CCEMT-P. Some hold certificates as instructors in various fields and educational topics.

Flight Nurse

A flight nurse is a nurse specialized in patient transport in the aviation environment. The flight nurse is a member of an aeromedical evacuation crew on helicopters and airplanes, providing in-flight management and care for all types of patients. Other responsibilities may also include planning and preparing for aeromedical evacuation missions and preparing a patient care plan to facilitate patient care, comfort and safety. Flight nurses may obtain certification in Emergency Nursing (CEN), Flight Nursing (CFRN) or Critical Care (CCRN).

Civilian Flight Nurses

Civilian flight nurses may work for hospitals, federal, state, and local governments, private medical evacuation firms, fire departments or other agencies. They have training and medical direction that allows them to operate with a broader scope of practice and more autonomy than many other nurses. Some states require that flight nurses must also have paramedic or EMT certification to respond to pre-hospital scenes.

Military Flight Nurses

A military flight nurse performs as a member of the aeromedical evacuation crew, and functions as the senior medical member of the aeromedical evacuation team on Continental United States (CONUS), intra-theater and inter-theater flights—providing for in-flight management and nursing care for all types of patients. Other responsibilities include planning and preparing for aeromedical evacuation missions and preparing a patient positioning plan to facilitate patient care, comfort and safety.

Flight nurses evaluate individual patient's in-flight needs and request appropriate medications, supplies and equipment, providing continuing nursing care from originating to destination facility. They act as liaison between medical and operational aircrews and support personnel in order to promote patient comfort and to expedite the mission, and also initiate emergency treatment for in-flight medical emergencies.

Task 1
(1) How many kinds of medical personnel are mentioned in the article?
(2) What are the job responsibilities of each category of medical personnel?

Task 2
Do you think medical personnel are important for civil aviation services? Why?

Unit 6 Safety and Emergencies

TAXI

1. Warm-up: discuss in pairs and answer the following questions.

I. What happened to the aircraft in the picture?

II. Do you agree or disagree that in an on-board emergency, safety is the top priority?

III. Complete the crossword puzzle with the given words and clues.

	ACROSS	DOWN
	(2) Please put on your life_____ immediately.	(1) Irregular and violent motion of air.
	(4) Make less nervous.	(3) An sudden and dangerous situation.
	(6) Hold tightly.	(5) Now it's time to witness the_____.
	(8) Loss of air pressure in the cabin.	(7) Each and every plane accident will result in a huge_____.
	(8) The part of a plane that keeps it move.	
	(10) The escape raft will_____ on the sea.	

jacket   miracle   grab   turbulence   engine
relax   loss   emergency   float   decompression

2. Spot: match the instructions A-F with the pictures. W

A. remain the brace position   B. put on the oxygen mask
C. open the emergency exit   D. put on your life vest
E. fasten your seatbelt   F. jump onto the slide

____A____

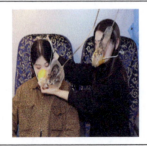

_____

_____

_____   _____   _____

3. Brainstorm: what other rules should you obey when emergency happens?

e.g. Follow the floor lighting.

4. Converse: work with a partner and discuss some emergencies that might happen on board and discuss the possible difficulties for flight attendants in managing the cabin in case of such emergencies.

TAKE-OFF

5. Complete the conversation using the words below.

located	experiencing	aircraft	whistle	straps
inflate	upset	tab	attention	life jacket

Flight Attendant: Excuse me, did you call, sir?
Passenger: Yes. I'm a little __(1)__ . I want to know what's happening?
Flight Attendant: As the captain said, our plane is __(2)__ some serious turbulence. You have to put on your __(3)__ immediately.
Passenger: I'm sorry. I didn't pay attention to the safety demonstration. Can you show me again?

Unit 6 Safety and Emergencies

Flight Attendant: Sure. Your life jacket is __(4)__ under your seat. Did you get it?
Passenger: Got it.
Flight Attendant: OK. Now pull the __(5)__ to open the pouch and take it out. Then put it over your head.
Passenger: Yep.
Flight Attendant: Now fasten the buckles and pull the __(6)__ tight around your waist. To __(7)__ the jacket, pull down this red cord, but don't inflate it until you leave the __(8)__. Are you clear?
Passenger: Yes, you've made it very clear.
Flight Attendant: Good. One more thing, you can use the __(9)__ and light to attract __(10)__ just in case of a water landing.
Passenger: All right. Thank you.

6. Give instructions about dos and dont's.

Match the verbs with the phrases to complete the instructions used in emergencies.

A. Pull   (1) the emergency exit.
B. Remain   (2) any personal belongings with you.
C. Breathe   (3) your seat!
D. Adopt   (4) normally.
E. Sit   (5) down!
F. Keep   (6) a mask towards your face.
G. Open   (7) the trolley in the galley.
H. Secure   (8) seated.
I. Don't take   (9) the brace position.
J. Don't leave   (10) your seatbelt fastened.

7. Listen and learn.

I. Listen to the conversations and mark the sentences True (T) or False (F).

Conversation (1)
① The captain has switched on the seatbelt sign.   (   )
② The woman hasn't fastened her seatbelt.   (   )

Conversation (2)
① Someone was smoking in the lavatory   (   )
② The smoke detector didn't go off.   (   )

Conversation (3)
① Both the aircraft engines failed to work.   (   )
② The flight attendant managed to reassure the anxious passenger.   (   )

56

II. Listen again and complete the sentences.
(1) Excuse me, madam. The captain has_____on the seatbelt sign.
(2) Madam, you_____return to your seat and strap in now!
(3) The smoke detector in the lavatory _____.
(4) I thought someone might have smoked in the _____.
(5) The flight is really_____.
(6) Don't worry. We will_____the safety of the passengers.

CLIMB

8. Explore and learn: in all emergencies, cabin crew must give the information and instructions to reassure the passengers. Match the concerns of passengers and the proper response.

Passenger concerns	Flight attendant responses/instructions
A. My wife has just fainted!	(1) Of course not. We are very safe.
B. Are we going to crash?	(2) Don't worry. Let me take care of her. She will be fine.
C. Why is the lavatory always occupied?	(3) I'm sorry, sir. You can use the one in business class. Come with me.
D. I'm starving!	(4) There's nothing to worry about. Everything is fine.
E. I'm really scared!	(5) Just breathe slowly and deeply. You'll be fine, sir.
F. I am out of breath.	(6) I'm sorry, sir. We will be serving lunch in about 15 minutes. Can I give you some refreshments first?

9. Language focus: time clauses.

(1) Before landing, the cabin crew will do safety checks.
(2) After the oxygen mask dropped down automatically, the passenger put it on immediately.

(3) Once the air pressure changed, the oxygen mask would drop down automatically.
(4) Keep your seatbelt fastened until further informed.
(5) As soon as we arrived at Hangzhou, an ambulance waited at the parking apron.

I. Reorder the words to make sentences.

(1) don't until inflate leave you the life jacket
  Don't inflate the life jacket until you leave the cabin.

(2) be we'll meals half an hour after serving
_____

(3) can move the cabin around the fasten seatbelt sign you once is off
_____

(4) seated until remain the aircraft stops
_____

10. Pronunciation: emphatic stress.

I. Listen and repeat the sentences. Notice how stress and a higher pitch are used to express strong opinions.

(1) Please get out immediately!
   *
(2) Put on the mask over your mouth and nose!
(3) Don't inflate the life jacket in the cabin!
(4) I'm terribly sorry for my mistake!
(5) Don't panic!
(6) Get the extinguisher!
(7) Don't open the emergency exit!
(8) Keep your mask on!
(9) Breathe normally.
(10) Stay calm!

II. Mark the stress by putting a "*" on the sentences and practise.

III. Write four sentences using these words. Then take turns reading them. Pay attention to the emphatic stress.

fantastic	ridiculous	terrible	amazing

11. Brainstorm: what other emergencies might take place on board?

e.g. cabin caught fire	

12. Master and practise.

I. Listen and try to complete the announcement in case of emergency.

Ladies and gentlemen, this is an __(1)__ announcement. This is an emergency announcement. We are experiencing a drop of cabin air __(2)__. Please stay in your seats with your seatbelts securely __(3)__. When your oxygen masks __(4)__ drop down, please remain calm and follow these instructions. To start the flow of oxygen, __(5)__ the mask towards you, put it firmly over your mouth and nose and tighten the __(6)__ behind your head. Repeat, pull it down and put it over your nose and mouth and breathe __(7)__. Make sure your own __(8)__ is worn properly before helping others.

Ladies and gentlemen, don't __(9)__. We are very safe. Please remain calm and keep your masks on until further __(10)__.

II. Listen again to these parts of the announcement and practise saying them.

(1) Ladies and gentlemen, this is an emergency announcement. This is an emergency announcement.

(2) Please stay in your seats with your seat belts securely fastened.

(3) Ladies and gentlemen, don't panic. We are very safe. Please remain calm and keep your masks on until further informed.

III. Work with a partner and practise making the announcement. First read it aloud then try to remember it and say it from memory.

CRUISE

13. Read and think: read the following passage and complete the tasks.

Southwest Airlines Engine Incident

Passengers on board a Southwest Airlines plane screamed, cried and vomited during an attempted landing in a storm in New Orleans.

The harrowing incident on Southwest Airlines Flight 3461 on Saturday also prompted one passenger to send goodbye texts to loved ones as the pilot attempted to land the plane.

"It was going all over the place. People were screaming, people were crying. The flight attendants were yelling over the speakers to fasten seatbelts as tightly as possible and I was texting my family goodbye," she added in comments carried by UK newspaper *The Daily Mail*. "I just don't understand why Southwest Airlines put everyone in that situation."

Another passenger, Marie Wary said she felt like she was about to die as the plane attempted to land, while at least one passenger vomited during the incident.

> "I thought we were going to crash."
> —— Lauren Bale

After attempting to land at Armstrong International Airport in New Orleans, the plane was redirected to Panama City, in Florida, where it refueled and later continued on with its journey—eventually landing safely.

But given the storm, there were questions over why the flight was not canceled before taking off, rather than trying to fly through the bad weather. Passengers said there was little to no visibility with thunder and lightning during the attempted landing.

In a statement, Southwest Airlines said: "Our top focus is Safety. Flight 3461 from Fort Lauderdale to New Orleans arrived about four hours behind schedule after persistent thunderstorms over New Orleans forced prolonged holding near New Orleans awaiting clearance from air traffic controllers followed by a refueling stop in Panama City before the completion of the journey." "The Safety of our Customers and Employees as well as the Safe operation of every flight is our highest priority," the statement added.

Task 1

According to the passage, did the flight attendant do the right thing during the incident?

Task 2

Decide if the statement is true (T), false (F) or not mentioned (NM).

(1) The incident occurred on Delta Airlines.	
(2) When the incident happened, cabin crew asked passengers to fasten the seatbelts.	
(3) No one vomited during the incident.	
(4) The flight was not canceled due to the invisible storm.	
(5) Safety is the top priority of the airlines.	

Unit 7 Descent, Landing and Layover

TAXI

1. Warm-up: discuss in pairs and answer the following questions.

I. What do passengers usually want to do when the aircraft has landed?

II. How do flight attendants feel at the end of the flight?

III. Complete the crossword puzzle with the given words and clues.

ACROSS	DOWN
(3) Put awag	(1) Reach a destination.
(5) Not exactly.	(2) The action of bringing an aircraft down to the ground.
(7) Plane_____ for the most part of the flight.	(3) Sir, you can take the_____ bus to Terminal 2.
(8) Go down.	(4) Tell someone of the danger.
(9) Sir, you cannot use your phone now as the plane is still_____.	(6) Make sure.

landing   descent   arrival   taxi   cruise
stow   warn   ensure   Shuttle bus   approximately

2. Spot: match the sentences A-F to the pictures.

A. Make sure your seatbelt is fastened.
B. Please return the remaining cups to us.
C. Be careful when opening the overhead bin.
D. Ensure your cellphone is in flight mode.
E. Please remain seated.
F. Please take all your belongings with you.

(1)____C____   (2)_____   (3)_____

Unit 7 Descent, Landing and Layover

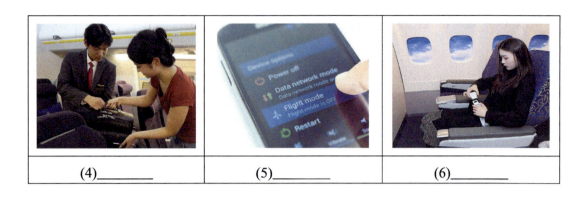

| (4)_____ | (5)_____ | (6)_____ |

3. Brainstorm: what other aspects should passengers pay attention to during landing?

e.g. put the seatback into the upright position

4. Converse: work with a partner and try to give safety warnings during landing.

TAKE-OFF

5. Complete the conversation using the words below.

pass	adjust	tray
stow	landing	armrest

Flight Attendant: Excuse me, sir. We are_____soon. Would you please set your seat back to the upright position and_____your_____table?
Passenger: Sorry, but I haven't finish my coke yet.
Flight Attendant: I see. Would you please_____the cup to me?
Passenger: Sure. There you go. Can you show me how to_____the seat back?
Flight Attendant: No problem. Just press the button on your_____.
Passenger: Thank you!
Flight Attendant: You are welcome.

6. Before landing flight attendants will make final checks.

I. Have a look at the final check routines and put them in a chronological order.

(1) Check seatbelts are securely fastened.
(2) The lavatory is locked.
(3) Passengers' personal belongings are stowed in the overhead compartments or under the seats.
(4) Tray tables are stowed and seat backs are upright.
(5) Complete the log.
(6) Buckled up for landing.
(7) Final clearance.
(8) Remind passengers to switch off electronic devices.
(9) Signal "cabin secure".
(10) Check again that your mobile phones are switched into flight mode.

30 min before landing	15 min before landing	3 min before landing
(1)		

II. Look at the situations below and use the verbs in the brackets to make polite requests.

(1) tray table down (stow)
Please stow the tray table.

(2) iPad in use (switch off)
_____

(3) seatback reclined (put up)   (4) seatbelt not fastened (buckle up)
_____   _____

(5) carry-on baggage in the aisle (put away)   (6) empty immigration form (fill in)
_____   _____

7. Listen and learn.

I. Listen to the conversations and mark the sentences True (T) or False (F).

Conversation (1)
① The lady wants to use the lavatory. ( )
② The flight attendant asked her to return to her seat. ( )

Conversation (2)
① The man wants to know the local time. ( )
② It is a quarter past five in the morning in London. ( )

Conversation (3)
① The man is using his cellphone during landing. ( )
② The flight attendant asked him to turn it off. ( )

II. Listen and complete the sentences.
(1) I'm sorry. For safety reasons, the lavatories have to be_____before landing.
(2) The plane is_____soon.
(3) Can you tell me what the_____time is in London now?
(4) Well, I'll_____my watch.
(5) Please turn off your_____.
(6) Just a_____, I'll switch it off soon.

CLIMB

8. Explore and learn: permission, obligation and prohibition.

Language Box

Permission	Obligation	Prohibition
You can stow your bag under the seat in front of you.	You have to switch off your mobile phone during take-off and landing.	You can't leave your bags in the middle of the aisle.
You're allowed to use laptop during the flight.	You've got to open the window shade during take-off and landing.	You aren't allowed to open the overhead compartment during taxiing.

I. Match these rules to the correct sign.

(1) No smoking on board.
(2) No food and drinks in the classroom.
(3) Fasten your seatbelt.
(4) Don't open the emergency exit unless it's necessary.

II. Pair work: use the language in the language box to take turns talking about each sign.

9. Language focus: study the phrasal verbs with pronouns.

Rewrite the instruction using a pronoun instead of the noun.
(1) Please switch off your cell phone.
   Please switch it off.
(2) Please fold away your tray table.
___
(3) Please stow your belongings in the overhead compartment.
___
(4) Please turn off your laptop immediately.
___
(5) Please open the window shade.
___
(6) Please put your armrest down.
___

10. Pronunciation: Intonation in questions.

I. Listen and repeat the questions. Notice how the intonation changes at the end of the yes/no questions and the open questions.

(1) Excuse me, what's the time difference between Beijing and London?

(2) Would you please show me how to adjust the seatback?
(3) Do you know how long it takes from terminal 1 to terminal 3?
(4) Have you secured the trolley in the galley?
(5) Have we completed the final checks?
(6) Could you please fasten your seatbelt?

II. Mark the different intonations with "↗" for tone up, "↘" for tone down and "*" for stress. Practise the intonations.

11. Master and practise.

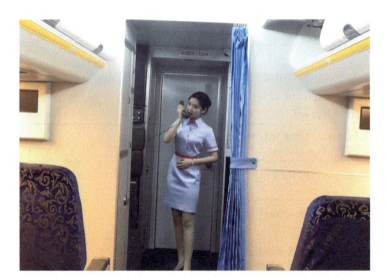

I. Listen and try to complete the pre-landing announcement.

Ladies and gentlemen, we_____for the delay. We'll be arriving at London Heathrow Airport for approximately fifteen minutes. The "fasten seat belts" sign has been_____. For your safety and the safety of other passengers, please_____seated and strap in. Please make sure your belongings are safely secured in the_____or under the seat in front of you. Please also make sure your tray table is_____properly and your seat back is upright.

For safety reasons, may we remind you that all electronic devices including mobile phones, laptops, tablet PCs should be_____until the "fasten seatbelts" sign is off and the _____on board will be suspended.

We hope that you've enjoyed our in-flight_____system and in preparation for_____ the system will be shut down. Please have your used_____ready for collection as the flight attendants go through the cabin.

Thank you for your cooperation.

II. Listen again to these parts of the announcement and practise saying them.

(1) We'll be arriving at London Heathrow Airport for approximately fifteen minutes.

(2) Please make sure your belongings are safely secured in the overhead compartment or under the seat in front of you.

(3) For safety reasons, may we remind you that all electronic devices including mobile phones, laptops, tablet PCs should be switched off until the "fasten seat belts" sign is off.

III. Work with a partner and practise making the announcement. First read it aloud then try to remember it and say it from memory.

CRUISE

12. Read and think: read the following passage and complete the tasks.

Malaysia Aims to Double Its Airport Capacity by 2040

Malaysia Airports Holdings plans to double Kuala Lumpur International Airport's capacity as it seeks a bigger slice of the 2.1 billion more passengers expected in Asia Pacific in the next two decades.

The company is looking to raise the capacity to 150 million, from the current 75 million, in the next 10 to 20 years, Raja Azmi Raja Nazuddin, chief financial officer of Malaysia Airports, said in an interview on the outskirts of the capital Kuala Lumpur on

Tuesday. The main terminal could reach full capacity in the next two years, he said.

"Don't hold your breath, though. Planning to revamp Kuala Lumpur's airport could last another two years, and it's unclear where the money will come from."

—Sean O'Neill

Kuala Lumpur joins neighboring cities Bangkok and Singapore in looking to expand airport capacity as routes in Asia Pacific are set to become among the world's busiest, according to the International Air Transport Association.

Malaysia's tourism board is targeting foreign visitor arrivals of 36 million by 2020, a 39 percent increase from last year.

Malaysia Airports sees passenger traffic across the airports it manages rising 6.3 percent this year as it banks on easier visa approvals for visitors from China and India.

The company is also looking to Hajj pilgrimages for more traffic and is cooperating with Malaysia Airlines, which provides chartered flights for the annual gathering, Raja Azmi said.

Improving services is a focus for the company, whose ranking in the Airport Service Quality survey fell to 12th in 2017, from ninth the previous year, he said. In 2018, Malaysia Airports is seeking to be back among the top 10.

As part of its five-year plan to diversify earnings, the company sets up an international unit that will focus on managing or buying stakes in airfields in the Middle East and Asia. It currently operates airports in Turkey and Qatar.

Task 1

According to the passage, why does the company want to expand its airport?

Task 2

Decide if the statement is true (T), false (F) or not mentioned (NM).

(1) Malaysia Airports Holdings plans to expand Kuala Lumpur International Airport.	
(2) Routes in Asia Pacific are believed to become the busiest among the world.	
(3) Malaysia's tourism board is targeting at European travelers.	
(4) Improving services is a focus for the company at present.	
(5) Ranking of the airport fell to 13th in 2017.	

Unit 8 Getting a Job

TAXI

1. Warm-up: discuss in pairs and answer the following questions.

I. Look at the pictures below. Which airline company does each of the logos represent? Which airline company do you want to work for?

II. Why do you want to work for this airline company? How much do you know about it?

III. Complete the crossword puzzle with the given words and clues.

ACROSS	DOWN
(3) A route of flight.	(1) Your_____ is about what type of person you are.
(8) Advantage.	(2) Honesty is a good_____ .
(9) Things you like doing.	(4) The book is boring and I have lost my_____ finishing it.
(10) I have_____with my homework.	(5) You have to prepare for the_____ if you want to get the job.
	(6) Come in and_____ yourself for a start.
	(7) I just graduated from college and don't have any work_____ .

introduce   airline   experience   personality   interview
quality   hobby   interest   strength   difficulty

2. Spot: match the interview question with the answer.

A. What is your hobby?	B. What do you think will be the most difficult part of the job?
C. What is the most important quality for this job?	D. Give us three key words about your personality.
E. Have you had any similar work experience?	F. Why do you choose our company?

Air China has always been the dream company that I want to get in.	I guess I would go for patient, enthusiastic and considerate.	In my opinion, it is important to be compassionate when serving passengers.
(1) __F__	(2) _____	(3) _____
I have experiences volunteering for various ceremonies and conferences, although strictly speaking, they are not work experiences.	I love all kinds of sports, especially jogging.	I think the major difficulty will be when passengers refuse to cooperate with us.
(4) _____	(5) _____	(6) _____

3. Brainstorm: what other questions might the interviewer ask you?

e.g. Please introduce yourself.

4. Converse: work with a partner. Choose one of the interview questions from the list and try to answer it.

TAKE-OFF

5. Introduce yourself.

I. For the items in the table, which ones do you think matter and which ones don't? Tick the ones that you think should be covered in your self-introduction.

	Items	
☐	qualifications and certificates	e.g. *I have passed TEM-4 this year and am certified in performing CPR and trauma first aid.*
☐	marriage and relationship	
☐	university major	

Items		
☐	society work	
☐	expectations for the jobs	
☐	weakness	
☐	favorite TV show	
☐	career plans	
☐	parents' occupations	
☐	language capabilities	

II. How would you introduce the ticked items? Organize your answer with reference to the given example.

6. Listen and learn.

I. Listen to the dialogues and number the pictures in order.
II. Listen again. How did the candidate answer the interviewer's question?

ANSWER:

(1) In my opinion, the most important quality for a flight attendant is patience.

(2) As far as I'm concerned, the most difficult part of the job is keeping calm in the case of an emergency.

(3) Yes, I agree. I believe teamwork is very important for flight attendants.

(4) I beg to differ. Keeping a good personal image is also a show of respect.

BUZZ: Pay attention to the headings that lead the sentences. Why do we add these adverbs when expressing opinions?

No._____
Answer_____

No._____
Answer_____

No._____

Answer_____

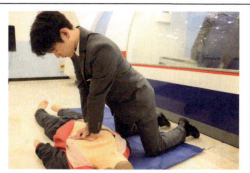

No._____

Answer_____

7. Explore and learn.

I. Choose the appropriate heading (e.g. in my opinion / as far as I'm concerned) and fill in the blanks.

II. Substantiate the answers with your own words in support of your opinions.

Conversation (1)
P: Do you think self-discipline is important for flight attendants?
C: (opinion)_____. (reasoning) _____
_____.

Conversation (2)
P: People say that being a flight attendant is a superficial job because he / she only cares about his / her looks.
C: (opinion)_____. (reasoning) _____
_____.

Conversation (3)
P: Passengers' need is always our priority. Do you agree or disagree?
C: (opinion)_____. (reasoning) _____
_____.

Conversation (4)
P: If you encounter a difficult passenger, what would you do?
C: (opinion)_____. (reasoning) _____
_____.

CLIMB

8. Getting to know the employer and the job.

I. For the items in the table, which ones do you think matter and which ones don't? Tick the ones that you think should familiarize yourself with before the interview.

	Items	
☐	salary	
☐	location	
☐	corporate history	
☐	employee benefits	
☐	corporate culture	
☐	vacations	
☐	on-the-job training	**e.g.** *I have passed TEM-4 and first aid test. But I hope to receive further trainings on the job.*
☐	key responsibilities	
☐	corporate finance	
☐	corporate values	

II. It is important to figure out what you expect to get from a job/employer before you actually go for the interview. Specify your expectations in the second column of the table with reference to the given example.

9. Pronounce: listen to the recording of the following answers and practise your pronunciation by repeating.

I. Mark the different intonations with "↗" for tone up, "↘" for tone down and "*" for stress. Practise the intonations.

II. Practise with your partner. Pay attention to the tones.
(1) In my opinion, it is important for a flight attendant to be patient with passengers.

(2) As far as I'm concerned, be compassionate is an indispensable quality for flight attendants.

(3) I believe the most difficult part of the job will be remaining calm even under emergent circumstances.

(4) I beg to differ. Being a flight attendant is not at all about looking good.

(5) I do have similar volunteering experiences. But to be honest, as a fresh graduate, I don't have work experience in this field.

(6) Air China is domestically renowned for being highly internationalized in its passenger composition.

10. Work in pairs: prepare a passage of self-introduction and read it to your partner. The partner should ask questions about the items covered in the introduction.

11. Brainstorm: what are the qualities you should exhibit during the interview? How do you convey these qualities to the interviewer?

Qualities	Conveying strategy
e.g. the willingness to help others	talking about how others' happiness makes you happy

12. Master and practise.

I. Listen to the conversation and decide if the statement is true (T) or false (F).

(1) Singapore Airlines have terrible and depressing services.	F
(2) US carriers are much better than those of Singapore Airlines.	
(3) The food served on a Singapore Airlines flight tends to be memorable.	
(4) The commentator thinks that the service of Singapore Airlines is worth its price.	
(5) United Airlines is a member of Star Alliance.	
(6) Mileage with United Airlines can be used to upgrade to Lufthansa, SAS and Qantas.	
(7) The in-flight service is poor in United Airline flights.	
(8) Economy Plus tickets provide passengers with extra legroom.	

II. Listen again. Complete the passage below.

The commentator discussed his ratings for two airline companies, namely _____. Overall, Singapore Airlines _____ than United Airlines. Singapore Airlines has _____ and it makes customers wish that they could choose it on every route no matter domestic or international. It is the first airline to _____. Apart from that, it has some of the best _____ _____. The _____ is far ahead of the competition, although _____ than most would like.

United Airlines is a _____ partner. The staff of the company _____, and the food and service on board _____ that offered by competing international carriers. The one advantage of the airlines is that it provides _____ with Economy Plus seating.

CRUISE

13. Read and think: read the following passage and complete the two tasks.

Airline Company Ratings

Airlines are not all the same. Some are obviously far better than others but this information has been hard to find. The following reviews of the major international airlines are based on industry reports, press coverage and passenger evaluations.

AIR FRANCE

A taste of European elegance from the time one boards, Air France cabin staff are often characterized as favoring passengers from home. Food, wine selections, and a generally well-regarded Business Class are plusses. Coach is, as with most carriers, something to endure. Changing planes at Charles de Gaulle is not for the faint of heart. Partner in the Sky Team with KLM. Overall service is regarded as superior to that offered on same routes by US carriers. Recent reports indicate noticeable improvements in Business and First Class services and amenities.

Overall Grade: B

ALITALIA

Avoid them, if possible, in coach. Their flight attendants don't think anyone should fly in any but the first ten rows of the aircraft. Coach service to Italy is indifferent. Strikes are an occasional problem. But the fact is, the Italians always do it with style, and most first-time Alitalia flyers come back saying "it really wasn't all that bad." Business Class service can be better than satisfactory based on your crew. Many Italy bound flights from the US are on 767 equipment. Flight attendants begin primping for their "walk through the airport on arrival" about an hour prior to landing.

Overall Grade: D

BRITISH AIRWAYS

Always reliable and a godsend in remote corners of the old Empire. Surprisingly good Business and First Class, consistently ranked among the best in the sky. Flat beds are now available on all long-haul flights. Planes are well maintained and communication from the flight deck is often characterized as "excellent." BA is sometimes taken for granted but its First Class is now rated among the world's best. Increasing luggage problems and delays at Heathrow are not a plus for those connecting to points in Europe. Some fly BA for the tea service—but there is so much more. Long-haul BA pilots are highly regarded.

Overall Grade: A-

Task 1

(1) Which company has the best overall rating? Which one has the worse?

(2) What aspects are examined by the commentator for this report? What are each company's strengths and weaknesses?

(3) You are preparing for an interview for Air China. How would knowledge about other airline companies help boost your performance?

Task 2

What is your dream airline company? How's its service as rated by passengers and commentators?

Appendix

Announcement for Practice

BEFORE TAKE-OFF

1. Baggage Arrangement

Ladies and gentlemen,

　　Welcome aboard ABC Airlines Flight CL1990. Please take your seat according to your seat number. Your seat number is on the edge of the rack. Please make sure your carry-on luggage is stored in the some small items can be put under the seat in front of you. Please take your seat as soon as possible to keep the aisle clear for others to go through.

　　Thank you!

2. Re-checking of Boarding Pass

Ladies and gentlemen,

　　Welcome aboard ABC Airlines Flight CL1990. We are flying to Beijing. The whole flight takes about 1 hour and 45 minutes. Would you please check your ticket and boarding pass again to make sure you're on the correct flight?

　　Thank you!

3. Restriction of Electronic Devices

Ladies and Gentlemen,

　　Welcome aboard ABC Airlines Flight CL1990. The cabin door has been closed. For your safety, please turn off your mobile phones and all electronic devices, or switch them to flight mode. Please don't use mobile phones during the whole flight. Laptop computers may not be used during take-off and landing. Please fasten your seatbelts, ensure that your tray table and seatback are in an upright position and open the window shades. This is a non-smoking flight. Please do not smoke on board. We wish you a pleasant trip.

　　Thank you for your cooperation.

4. Safety Demonstration

Ladies and Gentlemen,

　　We will show you the use of life vest, oxygen mask, seatbelt, and the location of the emergency exits. For your safety, please pay attention to our demonstration.

Your life vest is located under your seat. To put the vest on, slip it over your head. Then fasten the buckles and the straps tightly around your waist. Please don't inflate while in the cabin. You can pull the tabs down firmly to inflate before evacuation. If your vest needs further inflation, blow into the tubes on either side of your vest.

Your oxygen mask is stored in the compartment above your head, and it will drop automatically in case of an emergency. When the mask drops, pull it towards you to cover your mouth and nose, and slip the elastic band over your head, and then breathe normally.

Each chair has a seatbelt that must be fastened when you are seated. Please keep your seatbelt securely fastened during the whole flight. If needed, you may release the seatbelt by pulling the flap forward. You can adjust it as necessary.

There are eight emergency exits, two in the front of the cabin, two in the rear and four in the middle. The lights located on the floor will guide you to the exits if an emergency arises. For further information, please refer to the safety instruction card in the seat pocket in front of you.

Thank you!

5. Waiting for Orders from the ATC

Ladies and gentlemen,

This is your purser speaking. We just received the notice from the captain. Due to aircraft late arrival / unfavorable weather conditions / air traffic control / airport congestion / mechanical problems, we are now waiting for departure. Please remain seated and wait for a moment. If there is anything we can do for you, please let us know.

Thank you!

6. Apology for a Delay

Ladies and gentlemen,

I am the purser of this flight. On behalf of ABC Airlines, we extend the most sincere greetings to you. We are sorry for the brief delay due to aircraft late arrival / unfavorable weather conditions / air traffic control / airport congestion / mechanical problems.

Our team is looking forward to making your journey with us a safe and pleasant one. Thank you!

7. Air Conditioning Problems

Ladies and gentlemen,

We are now waiting for departure. You may feel a little bit hot now because the air conditioning system doesn't work well before take-off. We regret for this inconvenience at the moment. And you'll feel better after take-off.

Thank you!

8. Re-checking of Security

Ladies and gentlemen,

    We will takeoff shortly. For your safety, our flight attendants will check the cabin security, please turn off your mobile phones and all the electronic devices. Fasten your seatbelts, ensure that your tables and seatbacks are in an upright position and open the window shades.

    Thank you!

9. Takingoff Soon

Ladies and gentlemen,

    We will takeoff shortly. Please make sure that your seatbelts are securely fastened and keep your mobile phones switched off.

    Thank you!

AFTER TAKE-OFF

1. Ascending Notice

Ladies and gentlemen,

    This is your purser speaking. We are climbing now and we may encounter some turbulence. For your safety, please remain seated and fasten your seatbelts. According to regulations of CAAC, for safety considerations, we will provide cabin service 20 minutes after take-off. We will serve you soon.

    Thank you!

2. Food and Beverge Service

Ladies and gentlemen,

    In a few moments, the flight attendants will be serving meal / snacks and beverages. We hope you will enjoy them.

    For the convenience of the passenger seated behind you, please return your seatback to the upright position during our meal service. If you need any assistance, please feel free to ask.

    Thank you!

3. Turbulence

Ladies and gentlemen,

    We are encountering some turbulence. Please fasten your seatbelts. Please be careful of your food and drink. Lavatory is not to be used during turbulence. When you are using lavatory, please hold the handle tightly. During turbulence we will stop the cabin service.

    Thank you!

4. Flying at Night

Ladies and gentlemen,

To ensure a good rest for you, we will be dimming the cabin lights. If you wish to read, please turn on the reading light.

Because your safety is our primary concern, we strongly recommend you keep your seatbelts fastened throughout the flight.

Your cooperation in keeping the cabin quiet is appreciated. Should you need any assistance, please let us know.

Thank you!

BEFORE LANDING

1. 30 Minutes before Landing

Ladies and gentlemen,

We will be landing soon at Beijing Capital International Airport in about 30 minutes. The weather is rainy and outside temperature is 25 degrees Celsius. Please arrange all your belongings in advance and return your blankets to the flight attendants.

We are descending now. The lavatory has been closed. For your safety, please fasten your seatbelt, bring your seatback and tray table to the upright position and open the window shades. All electronic devices should be turned off.

During descent, your ears may feel uncomfortable because of the changing of cabin pressure. And you can overcome it by swallowing.

Thank you!

2. Security Check

Ladies and gentlemen,

We are descending now. Please take your seat and fasten your seatbelt. Seatbacks and tray tables should be returned to the upright position. If you are sitting beside a window, please help us by putting up the window shades. All laptop computers and electronic devices should be turned off at this time and please make sure that carry-on items are securely stowed. And for your safety, we kindly remind you that during the landing and taxiing, please do not open the overhead compartment.

Thank you!

3. Descending Notice

Ladies and gentlemen,

This is your purser speaking. We are descending now. For your safety, please sit down and fasten your seatbelts. Please keep your mobile phones powered off.

Thank you!

AFTER LANDING

1. Final Landing

Ladies and gentlemen,

We have just landed at Beijing Capital International Airport. The temperature outside is 25 degrees Celsius.

Please remain seated until our aircraft stops completely. When you disembark, please take all your belongings. Your checked baggage may be claimed in the baggage claim area. Passengers with connecting lights, please go to the transfer counter in the terminal.

Once again, we apologize for the delay of our flight. We thank you for your cooperation and understanding.

Thank you for choosing ABC Airlines. It has been a pleasure looking after you and we hope to see you again.

2. Disembarking from Air Bridge

Ladies and gentlemen,

Our plane has stopped at Terminal II of the airport. Please get your belongings ready and disembark through the front air bridge.

Thank you and good-bye!

3. Disembarking from Passenger Ramp

Ladies and gentlemen,

Please get your belongings ready and disembark through the front / rare passenger ramp. You can take the shuttle bus to the terminal building.

It's very slippery outside because of the rain. Please mind your step as you disembark.

Thank you and good-bye!

4. Waiting on Board

Ladies and gentlemen,

Passengers continuing to fly are requested to stay on board. We will take off shortly. Please don't leave the cabin and smoking is not permitted. If there is anything we can do for you, please let us know.

Thank you!

5. Waiting in the Terminal

Ladies and gentlemen,

Please take your boarding pass or ticket with you and wait for about 45 minutes in the terminal. You can leave large baggage and some small items like books and food on board.

We suggest you take all valuables and important documents with you. Please pay attention to the re-boarding announcement.

There will be a change of cabin crew here. On behalf of my team, I would like to wish you a pleasant journey. Thank you!

SPECIAL SITUATIONS

1. Delay

Ladies and gentlemen,

Due to air traffic control / airport congestion / unfavorable weather conditions / mechanical problems, we haven't been informed of the time of departure yet. Please wait for a moment until we have further information. We will be serving food and beverages while we are waiting for departure.

We apologize for the inconvenience. Thank you for your cooperation!

2. Alternate Airport

Ladies and gentlemen,

This is your purser speaking. We have just received the notice from the captain that due to bad weather we can't land at Beijing Capital International Airport. We are now flying to Tianjin Binhai International Airport. After 30 minutes, we will arrive at Tianjin Binhai International Airport. Our flight attendants will check the cabin security. Please fasten your seatbelts, ensure that your tables and seatbacks are in an upright position and open the window shades.

Thank you!

3. Detour Landing

Ladies and gentlemen,

We have just landed at Tianjin Binhai International Airport. Please keep your seatbelts fastened and remain seated until the plane has come to a complete stop. Please keep your mobile phones powered off. We'll have further information for you shortly.

Thank you!

4. Circling

Ladies and gentlemen,

This is your purser speaking. Due to unfavorable weather conditions at Beijing Capital International Airport, we have been ordered to circle over until we receive new instructions.

Thank you!

5. Return

Ladies and gentlemen,

  This is your purser speaking. We have just received notice from the captain and we are sorry to inform you that we will return to Hangzhou Xiaoshan International Airport due to maintenance matter. We expect to land at Hangzhou Xiaoshan International Airport at approximately 10:15.

  We apologize for any inconvenience. Your understanding will be very much appreciated.

6. Cancel and Stay Overnight

Ladies and gentlemen,

  We are very sorry to inform you that the flight has been canceled due to the temporary military ban along the route. We will have to stay overnight at airport. Please take all your belongings with you while leaving the plane.

  The plane will take off at 8 o' clock tomorrow morning.

  We apologize for any inconvenience. Your patience and understanding will be very much appreciated.

  Thank you!

7. Change of Aircraft

Ladies and gentlemen,

  May I have your attention, please? This is your purser speaking.

  We regret to inform you that we will have to transfer to another aircraft due to mechanical problem. Please take all your belongings when you disembark and follow our ground staff to the new aircraft.

  We apologize for any inconvenience. Your understanding and cooperation will be very much appreciated.

  Thank you!

8. Call for a Doctor

Ladies and gentlemen,

  May I have your attention, please?

  There is a sick passenger on board / There is a passenger who need to use prescription drug. If you are medical personnel, please identify yourself to any one of our cabin crew.

  Thank you!

EMERGENCY SITUATIONS

1. Fire in the Cabin

Ladies and gentlemen,

We have a minor fire in the front / center / rear cabin and we are quickly containing this situation. Please remain calm and follow the directions from your flight attendants. We will relocate the passengers near the fire. All other passengers remain seated with your seatbelts fastened.

Thank you for your cooperation and assistance.

2. Fire Extinguished

Ladies and gentlemen,

The fire has now been completely extinguished. The plane is cruising as scheduled and there will be no change in arrival time. We expect to land at Beijing Capital International Airport at 9:25.

We are sorry to have interrupted you and we thank you for your cooperation!
Thank you!

3. Decompression

Ladies and gentlemen,

Our airplane is now being depressurized. Please do not be panic. Remain in your seat with your seatbelt fastened. Please pull down one of the oxygen masks which have dropped from the ceiling! Place it over your nose and mouth and breathe normally. If you are seated next to a small child or infant, please put on your mask first and then assist your child. The aircraft will have an emergent descent. Please follow the instructions of cabin crew.

Thank you!

4. Emergency Landing

Ladies and gentlemen,

It is necessary to make an emergency landing. Our crew members are well trained for emergency situation. We will do everything necessary to ensure your safety. Please follow our instructions. After landing, please leave the aircraft as soon as possible.

Thank you!

Appendix — Announcement for Practice

Glossary

Unit 1

1. flight attendant — 乘务员
2. anticipate — v. [æn'tɪsɪpeɪt] 预计
3. cabin — n. ['kæbɪn] 机舱
4. earphone — n. ['ɪəfəʊn] 耳机
5. greet — v. [griːt] 问候
6. check — v. [tʃek] 检查
7. corridor — n. ['kɒrɪdɔː] 走廊
8. pre-flight — adj. [priː'flaɪt] 飞行前的
9. demonstration — n. [demən'streɪʃ(ə)n] 演示
10. luggage — n. ['lʌgɪdʒ] 行李
11. direction — n. [dɪ'rekʃn] 方向
12. lavatory — n. ['lævət(ə)rɪ] 厕所；洗手间
13. identify — v. [aɪ'dentɪfaɪ] 确定；识别
14. difficulty — n. ['dɪfɪk(ə)ltɪ] 困难
15. location — n. [lə(ʊ)'keɪʃ(ə)n] 地点
16. front — n. [frʌnt] 前方
17. aisle — n. [aɪl] 走廊
18. emergency — n. [ɪ'mɜːdʒ(ə)nsɪ] 紧急情况
19. row — n. [rəʊ] 排
20. fasten — v. ['fɑːs(ə)n] 扣紧
21. tighten — v. ['taɪt(ə)n] 使变紧
22. fold — n. [fəʊld] 折叠
23. switch — v. [swɪtʃ] 开关
24. stow — v. [stəʊ] 放置
25. adjust — v. [ə'dʒʌst] 调整
26. upright — adj. ['ʌpraɪt] 竖直的
27. position — n. [pə'zɪʃn] 方位
28. polite — adj. [pə'laɪt] 有礼貌的
29. request — v. [rɪ'kwest] 要求；请求
30. welcome — v. ['welkəm] 欢迎
31. overhead bin — 舱顶行李箱

Unit 2

1. routine — n. [ruː'tiːn] 例行公事

2. take-off 起飞
3. safety instruction card 安全说明书
4. blanket n. ['blæŋkɪt] 毛毯
5. seatbelt n. [siːtbɛlt] 安全带
6. laptop n. ['læptɒp] 笔记本电脑
7. headrest n. ['hedrest] 头靠
8. boarding pass 登机牌
9. secure adj. [sɪ'kjʊə] 安全的
10. delay v. [dɪ'leɪ] 延期；延误
11. footrest n. ['fʊtrest] 脚凳
12. refreshment n. [rɪ'freʃm(ə)nt] 点心
13. nervous adj. ['nɜːvəs] 紧张不安的
14. passenger n. ['pæsɪndʒə] 旅客
15. pregnant adj. ['pregnənt] 怀孕的
16. elderly adj. ['eldəlɪ] 上了年纪的
17. couple n. ['kʌp(ə)l] 夫妇
18. air-conditioner n. ['eəkəndɪʃənə(r)] 空调
19. heated adj. ['hiːtɪd] 热的
20. knob n. [nɒb] 旋钮
21. spare adj. [speə] 空余的
22. repeated adj. [rɪ'piːtɪd] 再三的
23. connection n. [kə'nekʃn] 连接
24. cracked adj. [krækt] 破裂的
25. temperature n. [temprətʃə(r)] 温度
26. cabin n. ['kæbɪn] 客舱
27. brief adj. [briːf] 简短的
28. introduction n. [ɪntrə'dʌkʃ(ə)n] 介绍
29. towel n. ['taʊəl] 毛巾
30. call button 服务铃；呼唤铃
31. announcement n. [ə'naʊnsm(ə)nt] 广播
32. regulation n. [regjʊ'leɪʃ(ə)n] 规则
33. reduce v. [rɪ'djuːs] 减少
34. fatigue n. [fə'tiːg] 疲劳
35. overweight adj. [əʊvə'weɪt] 超重的
36. insomnia n. [ɪn'sɒmnɪə] 失眠症
37. tiredness n. ['taɪədnis] 疲倦
38. overcome v. [əʊvə'kʌm] 克服
39. jet lag 时差感，飞行时差反应
40. caffeine n. ['kæfiːn] 咖啡因

Unit 3

1. arrival n. [ə'raɪv(ə)l] 到达

2. request   n. [rɪ'kwest] 要求
3. baggage   n. ['bægɪdʒ] 行李
4. drop   v. [drɒp] 掉下来
5. comfortable   adj. ['kʌmftəbl] 舒适的
6. compartment   n. [kəm'pɑːtm(ə)nt] 隔间
7. waste   n. [weɪst] 垃圾
8. problem   n. ['prɒbləm] 问题
9. fix   v. [fɪks] 修理
10. turn on/off   打开/关闭
11. turn up/down   调大/调小
12. put down/back   放下/收回
13. relax   v. [rɪ'læks] 放松
14. headphone   n. ['hedfəʊn] 耳机
15. newspaper   n. ['njuːzpeɪpə] 报纸
16. snack   n. [snæk] 零食
17. destination   n. [ˌdestɪ'neɪʃ(ə)n] 目的地
18. calm down   使……平静
19. dangerous   adj. ['deɪndʒərəs] 危险的
20. queue   v. [kjuː] 排队
21. instruct   v. [ɪn'strʌkt] 指示
22. offer   v. ['ɒfə] 提出，提供

Unit 4

1. soft drink   软饮料；不含酒精的饮料
2. steak   n. [steɪk] 牛排
3. brownie   n. ['braʊnɪ] 巧克力蛋糕
4. salad   n. ['sæləd] 色拉
5. alcohol   n. ['ælkəhɒl] 酒精；酒
6. butter   n. ['bʌtə] 黄油；奶油
7. roll   n. [rəʊl] 卷；卷形物
8. yogurt   n. ['jəʊgət] 酸奶酪；酸奶
9. dessert   n. [dɪ'zɜːt] 餐后甜点
10. ice-cream   n. ['aɪs'kriːm] 冰激凌
11. broccoli   n. ['brɒkəlɪ] 花椰菜；西兰花
12. cheese   n. [tʃiːz] [食品] 奶酪；干酪
13. french fries   法式炸薯条；炸土豆片
14. spinach   n. ['spɪnɪdʒ] 菠菜
15. steam   v. [stiːm] 蒸，散发；用蒸汽处理
16. grill   v. [grɪl] 烧，烤
17. roast   v. [rəʊst] 烤，焙；烘，烘烤
18. fry   v. [fraɪ] 油炸；油煎
19. boil   v. [bɒɪl] 煮沸，烧开

20.	vegetarian	adj. [ˌvedʒɪ'teərɪən] 素食的
21.	apologize	v. [ə'pɒlədʒaɪz] 道歉；辩解；赔不是
22.	turbulence	n. ['tɜːbjʊl(ə)ns] 骚乱，动荡；湍流，气流
23.	selection	n. [sɪ'lekʃ(ə)n] 选择，挑选；选集
24.	switch off	关掉；切断（电源）
25.	tray table	盘桌；小桌板
26.	complain	v. [kəm'pleɪn] 抱怨；控诉
27.	tremendous	adj. [trɪ'mendəs] 极大的，巨大的；惊人的；极好的
28.	client	n. ['klaɪənt] 客户；顾客；委托人

Unit 5

1.	medical	adj. ['medɪk(ə)l] 医疗的
2.	witness	v. ['wɪtnɪs] 见证
3.	fever	n. ['fiːvə] 发烧
4.	stomachache	n. ['stʌməkeɪk] 胃痛
5.	bleed	v. [bliːd] 流血
6.	stomach	n. ['stʌmək] 胃部
7.	heart attack	心脏病发作
8.	asthma	n. ['æsmə] 哮喘
9.	pain	n. [peɪn] 疼痛
10.	chest	n. [tʃest] 胸
11.	waist	n. [weɪst] 腰部
12.	knee	n. [niː] 膝盖
13.	ankle	n. ['æŋk(ə)l] 脚踝
14.	cramp	n. [kræmp] 痉挛，绞痛
15.	sore	n. [sɔː] 疼痛
16.	hurt	v. [hɜːt] 疼痛
17.	dizzy	adj. ['dɪzɪ] 眩晕的
18.	vitamin	n. ['vɪtəmɪn] 维生素
19.	aspirin	n. ['æsprɪn] 阿司匹林
20.	CPR mask	心肺复苏面罩
21.	oxygen mask	氧气面罩
22.	inhaler	n. [ɪn'heɪlə] 吸入器
23.	ice cube	冰块
24.	suggest	v. [sə'dʒest] 建议
25.	calf	n. [kɑːf] 小腿
26.	perform	v. [pə'fɔːm] 进行操作
27.	injure	n. ['ɪndʒə] 受伤
28.	bare	adj. [beə] 光的
29.	solid	adj. ['sɒlɪd] 固体的
30.	nap	n. [næp] 小憩
31.	unconscious	adj. [ʌn'kɒnʃəs] 无意识的

32.	relief	v. [rɪ'li:f] 解除（疼痛）
33.	take off	起飞；脱下
34.	indigestion	n. [ɪndɪ'dʒestʃ(ə)n] 消化不良
35.	panic	v. ['pænɪk] 慌张
36.	cruise	v. [kru:z] 平飞
37.	wound	n. [wu:nd] 伤口
38.	antiseptic wipe	消毒巾

Unit 6

1.	life jacket	救生衣
2.	miracle	n. ['mɪrək(ə)l] 奇迹
3.	grab	n. [græb] 抓住；攫取
4.	engine	n. ['endʒɪn] 发动机
5.	loss	n. [lɒs] 减少
6.	float	vt. [fləʊt] 使漂浮
7.	decompression	n. [di:kəm'preʃ(ə)n] 解压 降压
8.	life vest	n. 救生衣
9.	slide	v. [slaɪd] 滑动
10.	immediately	adv. [ɪ'mi:dɪətlɪ] 立即
11.	attention	n. [ə'tenʃ(ə)n] 注意力
12.	safety demonstration	安全演示
13.	pouch	n. [paʊtʃ] 小袋
14.	pull	vt. [pʊl] 拉；拔；拖
15.	personal	adj. ['pɜ:s(ə)n(ə)l] 个人的
16.	belongings	n. [bə'lɒŋɪŋz] 财产；所有物
17.	adopt	vt. [ə'dɒpt] 采取、采纳、采用
18.	trolley	n. ['trɒlɪ] 手推车
19.	galley	n. ['gælɪ] 飞机或船上的厨房
20.	brace position	防撞姿势
21.	aircraft	n. ['eəkrɑ:ft] 飞机
22.	anxious	adj. ['æŋ(k)ʃəs] 焦虑的
23.	strap in	拴上安全带
24.	smoke detector	烟雾报警器
25.	cigarette	n. [sɪgə'ret] 香烟
26.	trash bin	垃圾箱
27.	faint	v. [feɪnt] 晕厥
28.	crash	n. [kræʃ] 撞碎；坠毁
29.	occupied	adj. ['ɒkjʊpaɪd] 已占用的
30.	starving	adj. ['stɑ:vɪŋ] 饥饿的
31.	scared	adj. [skeəd] 害怕的
32.	breath	n. [breθ] 呼吸
33.	landing	n. ['lændɪŋ] 降落

34.	automatically	adv. [ɔːtə'mætɪklɪ] 自动地
35.	drop down	落下
36.	inflate	vt. [ɪn'fleɪt] 使充气
37.	panic	n. ['pænɪk] 恐慌
38.	normally	adv. ['nɔːm(ə)lɪ] 正常地
39.	calm	adj. [kɑːm] 平静的，镇定的
40.	incident	n. ['ɪnsɪd(ə)nt] 事件
41.	statement	n. ['steɪtm(ə)nt] 声明

Unit 7

1.	descent	n. [dɪ'sent] 下降
2.	layover	n. ['leɪəʊvə] 中断期间，中途短暂的停留
3.	climb	v. [klaɪm] 爬；攀登；上升
4.	stow	v. [stəʊ] 装载；收藏；使暂留；堆装；将某物收好
5.	warn	v. [wɔːn] 警告，提醒；通知
6.	ensure	v. [ɪn'ʃɔː] 保证，确保；使安全
7.	shuttle bus	班车（在较短距离之间往返的交通车）；豪华轿车
8.	approximately	adv. [ə'prɒksɪmətlɪ] 大约，近似地；近于
9.	cellphone	n. ['sel,fəʊn] 蜂窝式便携无线电话；手机
10.	remain	v. [rɪ'meɪn] 保持；依然；留下
11.	adjust	v. [ə'dʒʌst] 调整，使……适合；校准
12.	button	n. ['bʌtn] 按钮；纽扣
13.	chronological	adj. [krɒnə'lɒdʒɪk(ə)l] 按年代顺序排列的；依时间前后排列而记载的
14.	locked	adj. ['lɔkt] 上锁的
15.	upright	adj. ['ʌpraɪt] 垂直的，直立的；笔直的
16.	log	n. [lɒg] 记录；航行日志
17.	buckle up	系好安全带；把……扣紧
18.	clearance	n. ['klɪər(ə)ns] 清除；空隙
19.	switch off	（用开关）关掉；切断（电源）
20.	electronic devices	电子设备
21.	flight mode	飞行模式
22.	recline	v. [rɪ'klaɪn] 靠；依赖；斜倚
23.	carry-on baggage	随身行李
24.	immigration form	入境申请表
25.	permission	n. [pə'mɪʃ(ə)n] 允许，许可
26.	obligation	n. [ɒblɪ'geɪʃ(ə)n] 义务；职责；债务
27.	prohibition	n. [prəʊhɪ'bɪʃ(ə)n] 禁止；禁令
28.	capacity	n. [kə'pæsɪtɪ] 能力；容量
29.	decade	n. ['dekeɪd] 十年
30.	raise	v. [reɪz] 提高

Unit 8

1. company — n. ['kʌmp(ə)nɪ] 公司
2. introduce — v. [ɪntrə'djuːs] 介绍
3. airline — n. ['eəlaɪn] 航空公司
4. experience — n. [ɪk'spɪərɪəns] 经历
5. personality — n. [pɜːsə'nælɪtɪ] 个性
6. interview — n. ['ɪntəvjuː] 面试
7. quality — n. ['kwɒlətɪ] 品质
8. hobby — n. ['hɒbɪ] 爱好
9. interest — n. ['ɪnt(ə)rɪst] 兴趣
10. strength — n. [streŋθ] 强项
11. difficulty — n. ['dɪfɪk(ə)ltɪ] 困难
12. ceremony — n. ['serɪmənɪ] 典礼
13. conference — n. ['kɒnf(ə)r(ə)ns] 会议
14. qualification — n. [ˌkwɒlɪfɪ'keɪʃ(ə)n] 资质
15. certificate — n. [sə'tɪfɪkɪt] 证书
16. major — n. ['meɪdʒə] 专业
17. weakness — n. ['wiːknəs] 弱点
18. favorite — adj. ['feɪv(ə)rɪt] 最爱的
19. expectation — n. [ekspek'teɪʃ(ə)n] 期待
20. capability — n. [ˌkeɪpə'bɪlətɪ] 能力
21. patience — n. ['peɪʃ(ə)ns] 耐心
22. teamwork — n. ['tiːmwɜːk] 团队合作
23. image — n. ['ɪmɪdʒ] 形象
24. priority — n. [praɪ'ɒrɪtɪ] 优先，优先权
25. salary — n. ['sælərɪ] 工资
26. benefit — n. ['benɪfɪt] 福利
27. corporate culture — 企业文化
28. vacation — n. [və'keɪʃn] 假期
29. train — v. [treɪn] 训练
30. finance — n. [faɪ'næns] 财务
31. value — n. ['væljuː] 价值
32. service — n. ['sɜːvɪs] 服务

Audio Script

Unit 1 Pre-flight and Boarding

8. Listen and learn.

Dialogue 1: A passenger wanting to change seat when the cabin attendant is carrying out safety check.

C: Madam, please fasten your seatbelt. We'll be taking off soon.

P1: Yeah. Yeah… Sorry, it's just…

C: Yes, madam. How can I help?

P1: My husband sits over there. Can I move to sit next to him?

C: Madam, I'm sorry. The two seats next to your husband's are already taken. We'll have to ask the other two passengers. But we're about to take off very soon.

P1: Yes, but… but my husband has high blood pressure. I'm worried letting him sit there by himself. I need to make sure he's okay.

C: Okay, in that case…I see. I'll go and ask.

P2: I can change with your husband if you want.

P1: Oh! How kind of you! That'll be fantastic!

C: Thank you, sir. I'll go and bring your husband here. Please be assured, madam.

P1: Thank you so much!

Dialogue 2: There is a mother with two little children and two carry-on bags.

C: Welcome on board, madam. May I have a look at your boarding pass, please?

P: OK, just a second. There you go.

C: 16A, 16B and 16C. Yeah, it's right here, madam.

P: Yeah. Thanks. George, where are you going? It's our seat here. Gary, go and get your brother. Oh my goodness. Am I in the way? Sorry, I'll be quick. It's a mess…

(The mother is in the way of other passengers.)

C: Don't worry, madam. Allow me to help you with your luggage.

(The cabin attendant helps with the luggage.)

P: Oh, thank you so much. George! Come here. What did I tell you just now? Remember?

C: Madam, it's sorted out. Please keep an eye on your children. It's not safe having them wandering about when other passengers are stowing their luggage.

P: Yes, I will. Thanks a lot.

Dialogue 3: A passenger cannot find space for his baggage in the overhead stowage compartment, and is standing in the way of others.

C: Sir, can I help?

P: Yeah, there's no room for my guitar.

C: Can I help you with this? There's room at the back.

P: Oh, okay. Where is it?

C: Over there. Right above row 36.

P: Sounds good to me. Can you please take care not to place it upside down? Because it's kind of fragile.

C: Yeah, please be assured.

P: Thanks a lot.

Dialogue 4: A cabin attendant is handing out newspapers to passengers.

C: Today's *China Daily*, sir.

P: Thanks…Actually, do you have other English newspapers like *The New York Times*?

C: No, I'm afraid not, sir. Can I offer you anything else?

P: What else have you got?

C: Let's see. There's *The Wall Street Journal, Guardian, The Telegraph*…

P: Yep. I'll have *The Telegraph*, please.

C: Here you go, sir.

P: Thanks.

C: Enjoy your reading.

11. Pronounce: listen to the recording of the following sentences and practise your pronunciation by repeating.

(1) Could you please remain on your seat until I've checked with the passenger list?

(2) Could you please fasten your seatbelt and tighten it?

(3) Could you please adjust your seatback to the upright position?

(4) Would you please wait for a second while I go and check if we have any left?

12. Master and practise.

(I- the interviewer, S- Sarah)

I: Okay. So you've told us a lot about, what you call it, the preflight procedures. That's before passengers board the plane. So what's it like when the actual boarding begins?

S: So five minutes before boarding we check the boarding music for the right volume. This music is played over the plane's loudspeaker system until five minutes before take-off but not during the flight.

Then the cabin crew have to meet and greet passengers as they come on board. We help them to find their designated seats.

I: That's like, you'll say stuff like "good morning", "good afternoon", "welcome on board", right?

S: Right. That's part of the greeting. And also this, "Can I have a look at your boarding pass, please?" Then passengers will show us their boarding passes and so we know where they sit. If it's a wide-body airliner, like Boeing 747, you know, with two aisles, we tell passengers on which one their seats locate. Right or left.

I: I see. So what happens then?

S: What often happens is that passengers will block the passage. It could be that they can't find their seat, or can't find enough space for bags, or don't know where to hang the coat, etc. So that's why we need our colleagues to be in the middle of the cabin to offer assistance. We help them with their hand luggage if they cannot manage themselves. We ask them to sit down as quickly as possible so those behind them can pass through.

I: Yeah, I guess everyone has been there, getting a little bit annoyed when the people in front of us just stand there right in the way.

S: Yes, you're quite right. Because for each flight, there will be different situations. Sometimes it could be more problematic because the boarding flow actually determines when we can take off. So honestly, the more, you know, "little situations" our passengers have, the more anxious we get. Sometimes these things can get on your nerves. But you'll have to keep smiling.

Unit 2 Routines after Take-off

8. Pronunciation: linked sounds

I. Listen and repeat the sentences.
(1) Excuse me, I think there's a problem with this headrest.
(2) Would it be OK for me to upgrade to business class?
(3) Would you turnoff your power bank?
(4) Could you please put it in the overhead compartment or stow it under the seat in front of you?

II. Mark the linked sounds in the sentences below. Listen and check, Then practise reading the sentences.
(1) I'm afraid that I don't understand English.
(2) The temperature in the cabin will drop as soon as the plane stops climbing.
(3) Give a brief introduction of the weather conditions at the destination.
(4) Let me get a wet towel for you.

11. Master and practise.

I. Listen to the captain's announcement and complete the announcement during take-off.

Ladies and gentlemen, this is your captain speaking. We have left Shanghai for Osaka. The distance is 1,350 kilometers and it takes about two hours. The cruising altitude is 9,500 meters. We are expected to arrive at Kansai International Airport at about 14:00 (local time). The weather today is very good, and I wish you all a pleasant journey with our airline. Thank you.

II. Listen to the purser giving further information to the passengers and complete the announcement.

Ladies and gentlemen, it's great to have you on board. In accordance with CAAC regulations, smoking is not allowed during the whole flight. There is a lunch service on today's flight. You can use the in-flight entertainment system throughout the flight. Duty free items are available for purchase shortly after the lunch. Please refer to the shopping on board magazine in the seat pocket in front of you.

Please remain seated and keep your seat belt fastened in case of sudden turbulence. If there is anything we can do for you, please press the call button and we will come to you right after.

We'll begin our meal service in about 15 minutes. This is a short flight, so please kindly look at the menu card in your seat pocket and have your orders ready. As the trolleys pass through the cabin, please keep the aisles clear. Thank you.

III. Listen again to parts of the announcement.

(1) Ladies and gentlemen, it's great to have you on board. In accordance with CAAC regulations, smoking is not allowed during the whole flight.

(2) Duty free items are available for purchase shortly after the lunch. Please refer to the shopping on board magazine in the seat pocket in front of you.

(3) Please remain seated and keep your seat belt fastened in case of sudden turbulence.

Unit 3 Passenger Comfort

6. Listen and learn.

Dialogue 1: explaining for a late arrival

P: Excuse me.

C: Yes. How can I help?

P: Can I ask what the time of arrival is?

C: Let's see. We'll be arriving at our destination in about an hour.

P: An hour? But it's supposed to be 14:35, no?

C: Yes, sir. I'm sorry but because there was half an hour's delay when we took off, we'll be arriving 15 minutes behind the schedule. I do apologize for any of the inconvenience it causes you.

P: OK, fine. I'll just take another nap then. Thanks.

Dialogue 2: an unsettled child

C: Madam, the captain is expecting some turbulence. You might want to put your child back on his seat and fasten his seat belt.

P: I'm sorry, but he's crying so bad.

C: I see, madam… I'll go and check if I can find anything to calm him down.

P: Yes, that's very kind of you.

C: No problem. I'll be quick.

(After a while)

C: Madam, we happen to have some cookies in the galley.

(Handing over the cookie to the lady)

P: Tommy, look! What we've got here.

(The child calming down)

C: Here, let me help him back to his seat.

P: Thank you so much.

C: You're welcome, madam.

Dialogue 3: a passenger wishing to open the baggage compartment

P: Hi there! Can you help?

C: Yes, sir. How can I help?

P: Could you please help me fetch my bag? It's in the compartment over 16C down there. A navy blue backpack. There was not enough space for my bag when I came, so I put it back there.

C: Sure, sir. Just a second.

(After a few minutes)

C: Sir, there you go.

P: Thank you so much.

C: You're welcome, sir. Anything else?

P: Oh, just a second, please. I'll just my stuff out and can you help me put this back again? I'm sorry for the bother but the window seat doesn't leave me much choice, plus these two gentlemen are fast asleep...

C: No worry, sir. I'll wait. Or if you wish, you can always put your bag underneath your seat.

Dialogue 4: a cold passenger

P: Excuse me. It's a bit cold here. Could you please turn the AC down a bit?

C: I'm sorry; sir. But the AC has to be kept on for the air circulation. I can bring you a blanket instead. Does that sound okay to you, sir?

P: OK, I see. Blanket will do I guess.

C: Thank you for your understanding. I'll be back in just a second.

(After a while)

C: Sir. Here you go.

P: Thank you, miss.

C: Anything else I can help with?

P: No, that's everything. You've been very helpful.

9. Pronounce: listen to the recording of the following answers and practise your pronunciation by repeating after.

(1) Don't worry, sir. It'll be fine.

(2) I see, madam. I'll go and check if I can find anything to calm him down.

(3) Let's see. We'll be arriving at our destination in about an hour, sir.

(4) Certainly, madam. That'll be my pleasure.

(5) I'm afraid not, sir. You'll have to fasten your seat belt now.

(6) I'm sorry, but I can bring you a blanket instead. Will that do for you, sir?

12. Master and practise.

C: Please buckle your seat belt, madam. Are you okay, madam?

P1: Emmm…

C: Are you okay, madam?

P1: No. I'm not well… It's too shaky. It's making me sick.

C: Madam. Madam. It's okay. Relax. Take a deep breath.

P1: Okay, I'm trying.

C: Madam, I'll go and get a towel and some ice cubes. Please keep taking deep breaths.

(After a while)

C: Madam, here's the towel. It would help if you place it on your forehead and the back of your neck.

P1: OK, thanks. I'm sorry but the baby there has been crying for like 20 minutes nonstop. It's making things worse. Can you please talk to the mother?

C: Certainly, madam. It seems the mother is already trying to sooth her baby. But I'll talk to her anyway.

C: Madam, can I help?

P2: I don't know. My baby won't stop crying. I think it's because his teddy bear was dropped underneath the seat just now. We couldn't find it no matter how.

C: I'll go and have a look if there's anything to cheer him up. You hold on here.OK?

P2: Thanks. That'll be great.

(After a while)

C: Madam. A colleague has a teddy bear key chain. So I borrowed it. Shall we have a try?

P2: Oh it might just work. Look Penny, look what I've got!

(P2 plays with the toy)

P2: I think he's happy now. Thank you so much. What's your name, please?

C: Call me Sarah.

P2: Thank you, Sarah.

C: My pleasure. We can also have a look around for Penny's bear after the plane has landed. I think it's just hiding underneath a seat. Don't worry.

P2: That's so kind of you.

Unit 4 Food and Drinks

5. Food on the meal tray.

I. Listen and label the objects on the meal tray.
(1) dessert / ice-cream
(2) pure water
(3) bread
(4) salad
(5) fork
(6) chocolate
(7) butter
(8) knife
(9) spoon
(10) chicken curry with broccoli

II. Listen again and complete the sentences.
(1) It's a little spicy.
(2) It's cooked with broccoli and cheese.
(3) There is also a roll with salted butter.

(4) It's chocolate brownie with ice-cream.
(5) Do you want brown sugar or white sugar?
(6) It's a bowl of vegetables.

7. Listen and learn.

I. Listen to the conversations. What does each passenger order and do they get what they want?

Conversation 1
FA: Excuse me, sir. Would you like something to eat?
Man: Sure.
FA: Today we have roasted chicken and fish curry.
Man: Chicken, please.
FA: There you go. What would you like to drink?
Man: A glass of whisky, please.
FA: OK.

Conversation 2
FA: Excuse me, madam. Would you like chicken or fish?
Woman: Oh, have you got any beef?
FA: No, I'm sorry. Our choices on today's flight are roasted chicken and fish curry.
Woman: Is the fish curry very spicy?
FA: No, it's just mildly spiced. Would you like to try it?
Woman: Good, I'll take the fish. Could I have a glass of water, please?
FA: Sure. Here you are.
Woman: Thank you.

Conversation 3
FA: Would you like beef or chicken, sir? Or the vegetarian option, the spinach lasagna?
Man: Lasagna, please.
FA: Here you are. What would you like to drink?
Man: What kind of fruit juice have you got?
FA: Apple, orange, pineapple and tomato.
Man: Apple juice, please.
FA: Here you are, sir.

II. Listen and complete the phrases of offering and ordering food.

Offering food
(1) Would you like something to eat?
(2) How about fish curry?
(3) May I offer you a drink madam?
(4) What would you like to have for lunch sir?

Making orders
(1) Do you have beef?
(2) Could I have a glass of pure water, please?

(3) Whisky on the rock, please.

(4) Black tea with milk, please.

Apologizing

(1) I'm sorry for having you waiting.

(2) I'm sorry that we've run out of the cheeseburger.

(3) I do apologize.

Giving the meal tray

(1) There you go, madam.

(2) Here you are, sir.

10. Pronounce: Intonation in questions of choice.

(1) Would you like to have mocha or cappuccino?

(2) Would you like your whisky straight or on the rock?

(3) How do you like your tea, weak or strong?

(4) We have a selection of soft drinks. Do you want Coke, Fanta or Spirit?

(5) How do you like your steak, rare, medium or well done?

(6) Green tea or black tea?

11. Master and practise.

Ladies and gentlemen, the fasten seatbelt sign has been switched off and you can move around the cabin. Our in-flight meal service will begin shortly so please watch out for the trolley. Please put down the tray table in front of you. We have three choices for the main course which are beef with potatoes, fish with rice and vegetable lasagna. Today's dessert is chocolate brownie. We offer a selection of hot and cold beverages including coffee, tea and soft drinks. Alcohol like wine, beer and cocktail are also available on board.

Please check the menu card in your seat pocket and have your order ready. Thank you and enjoy your flight.

Unit 5 Health and Medical Issues

6. Listen and learn.

Dialogue 1: fever

P: Excuse me. Can I have an extra sheet of blanket, please? It's so cold.

C: Sure, madam. Anything else I can help you with?

P: I don't know but I've got chills and my back is sore. My throat hurts also.

C: For how long exactly have you had these discomforts?

P: I'm not sure. I guess it's about an hour into the flight.

C: Madam, I think you might be having a fever. I would suggest you drink more hot water and keep yourself warm.

P: Yeah… You might be right.

C: Meanwhile, I'll go and see if we've got any antipyretics.

P: OK. Thank you very much.

Dialogue 2: faint

C: What happened? What's with the lady?

P: Oh gosh. She just fainted all of a sudden. Get some help, please!

C: Jack, a lady fainted here. We have to perform a CPR.

P: Madam, are you traveling with her?

C: No. I don't think she's got company.

P: OK. Can you please help me lay her down on the aisle and loose her shoes?

C: I get this.

Dialogue 3: indigestion

P: Tea, coffee, orange juice… Are you okay, madam?

C: No, not really… My stomach is not well. Must've been something I ate.

P: So how's it now? Have you got cramps? Or any pain? Or it's just the feeling of fullness?

C: Fullness. A little bit pain down here. It happens when I drink cold mild before a meal.

P: I see. I would suggest that you don't take in any solid food for an hour or so. I'll go and get a blanket for you to keep your tummy warm.

C: That's very kind of you. Thanks.

Dialogue 4: a cut on the head

P: Madam. What happened? You're bleeding.

C: I'm all right. A luggage dropped from above and hit me when I was trying to get my laptop…

P: Please. You must not touch the injured area with bare hand. It'll increase the chance of infection.

C: All right.

P: I'll ask my colleague to do the disinfection and dressing for you. Do you feel dizzy or nausea?

C: No. I'm all right.

P: Madam, I would suggest you sit down and lie back for a while. It'll help you settle.

9. Pronounce: Listen to the recording of the following answers and practise your pronunciation by repeating after.

(1) I'll get you a towel and a blanket. I would suggest that you keep yourself warm.

(2) I'll get you some anti-indigestion pills and hot water.

(3) I'll get you antiseptic wipes fir disinfection.

(4) Don't panic, madam. We've got crew member professionally trained to deal with this kind of emergencies.

(5) Please stay calm, sir.

(6) I would suggest that you don't take in any solid food for an hour or so.

12. Master and practise.

C1: What happened? Are you okay, sir?

P1: I…don't know. I felt this acute pain all of a sudden and when I looked, my leg was bleeding! I don't even know where I get this cut.

C1: Sir, do you have any pain now? Can I have a look at the wound? Sir, don't worry. We have a colleague experienced in treatment of physical trauma. Let's have a look.

C1: Hmmm. It's not so bad. I'll go and ask my colleague. Please remain on your seat. It won't be a second.

P: Please be quick. I hate blood. I'm feeling a bit dizzy. I… I'm losing blood.

(After a while)

C1: Sir. Hello? Hello? Sir. Can you hear me?

(The passenger is not responding.)

C1: Michael, a passenger fainted here. I guess it's blood phobia. Get me the CPR mask. Quick!

P2: Let me help. I'm a physician. I know how to do proper CPR.

C1: Oh thank god. Go ahead sir. I'll help you. Sir, madam, please we might need your help to lay this gentleman down on the aisle.

Unit 6 Safety and Emergencies

7. Listen and learn.

Conversation (1)

FA: Excuse me, madam. The captain has switched on the seatbelt sign. For your safety, you must return to your seat and strap in now!

Woman: I'm sorry. I'm going back to my seat now.

Conversation (2)

FA: Did you call, sir?

Man: Yes. The smoke detector in the lavatory went off just now. Could you go and check what is going on there?

FA: Thank you and I'll go right away.

(A few moments later)

FA: Excuse me, sir. I've just checked the lavatory. The sound you heard was not from the smoker detector. It was another passenger's alarm. Thank you for reminding us.

Man: Well, that's good. I thought someone might have smoked in the lavatory.

Conversation (3)

Woman: Excuse me, miss.

FA: Yes?

Woman: The flight is really bumpy. Is it safe?

FA: Don't worry. We will ensure the safety of the passengers.

Woman: OK.

10. Pronunciation: Emphatic stress.

(1) Please get out immediately!

(2) Put on the mask over your mouth and nose!

(3) Don't inflate the life jacket in the cabin!

(4) I'm terribly sorry for my mistake!

(5) Don't panic!

(6) Get the extinguisher!

(7) Don't open the emergency exit!

(8) Keep your mask on!
(9) Breathe normally.
(10) Stay calm!

12. Master and practise.

Ladies and gentlemen, this is an emergency announcement. This is an emergency announcement.We are experiencing a drop of cabin air pressure. Please stay in your seats with your seat belts securely fastened. When your oxygen masks automatically drop down, please remain calm and follow these instructions. To start the flow of oxygen, pull the mask towards you, put it firmly over your mouth and nose and tighten the elastic band behind your head. Repeat, pull it down and put it over your nose and mouth and breathe normally. Make sure your own mask is worn properly before helping others.

Ladies and gentlemen, don't panic. We are very safe. Please remain calm and keep your masks on until further informed.

Unit 7 Descent, Landing and Layover

7. Listen and learn.
Conversation (1)
Woman: Excuse me, miss. Can you unlock the lavatory?
FA: I'm sorry. For safety reasons, the lavatories have to be closed before landing.
Conversation (2)
Man: Can you tell me what the local time is in London now?
FA: It is a quarter past six in the morning in London.
Man: Thank you.
Conversation (3)
FA: Excuse me, sir. Please turn off your cellphone.
Man: Just a second. I'll switch it off soon.

10. Pronunciation: Intonation in questions.
(1) Excuse me, what's the time difference between Beijing and London?
(2) Would you please show me how to adjust the seatback?
(3) Do you know how long it takes from terminal 1 to terminal 3?
(4) Have you secured the trolley in the galley?
(5) Have we completed the final checks?
(6) Could you please fasten your seatbelt?

11. Master and practise.

Ladies and gentlemen, we apologize for the delay. We'll be arriving at London Heathrow Airport for approximately fifteen minutes. The "fasten seatbelts" sign has been switched on. For your safety and the safety of other passengers, please remain seated and strap in. Please make sure your belongings are safely secured in the overhead compartment or under the seat in front of you. Please also make sure your tray table is stowed properly and your seat back is upright.

For safety reasons, may we remind you that all electronic devices including mobile phones, laptops, tablet PCs should be switched off until the "fasten seatbelts" sign is off and the lavatories on board will be suspended.

We hope that you've enjoyed our in-flight entertainment system and in preparation for landing the system will be shut down. Please have your used headsets ready for collection as the flight attendants go through the cabin.

Thank you for your cooperation.

Unit 8 Getting a Job

6. Listen and learn: expressing opinions.

Dialogue 1: personal image

(A: Interviewer; B: Interviewee)

A: So here's the question for you. Some people think that being a flight attendant is all about looking good and dandy, which they regard as trivial. What do you think?

B: Hmmmm… I beg to differ. Keeping a good personal image is also a show of respect. It's the particularity of our profession.

A: So you think it's actually important?

B: Yes. We are in the service sector, in which customer experience is the utmost goal. Maintaining a good personal image is apparently a major contributor to the pleasantry of customers.

Dialogue 2: keeping calm

A: So, what do you think is the most important quality for a flight attendant?

B: As far as I'm concerned, the most difficult part of the job is keeping calm in the case of an emergency.

A: Why do you say so? Any examples in particular?

B: One scenario I can think of is that when the jet encounters turbulence, flight attendants must keep calm so that they will be cool enough to pamper passengers and make them stay put. Otherwise, if the flight attendants themselves panicked from the beginning, everything will fall into chaos.

Dialogue 3: patience

A: I've had a look at your CV. And now there are questions for you.

B: Yes.

A: What do you think is the most important quality for a flight attendant?

B: In my opinion, the most important quality for a flight attendant is patience.

A: Why so? Care for an elaboration?

B: Sometimes, the situation gets a little bit tricky and the passenger won't cooperate. It takes a lot of patience to persuade and comfort. It is always important that we, as employees of the service sector, know how to control our temper.

Dialogue 4: teamwork

A: Tell me what is your comment on this sentence and why you say so: Teamwork is important for flight attendants.

B: Yes, I agree. I believe teamwork is very important for flight attendants. Cabin crew works as a team. Most jobs require us to look after each other's back, not only to ensure maximum efficiency, but more importantly, to avoid mistakes.

A: Give an example for illustration, please.

B: The one off the top of my head is in emergencies. The cabin crew really need to stick together and cooperate with each other so that every action can be perfectly coordinated.

9. Pronounce: listen to the recording of the following answers and practise your pronunciation by repeating after.

(1) In my opinion, it is important for a flight attendant to be patient with passengers.

(2) As far as I'm concerned, be compassionate is an indispensable quality for flight attendants.

(3) I believe the most difficult part of the job will be remaining calm even under emergent circumstances.

(4) I beg to differ. Being a flight attendant is not at all about looking good.

(5) I do have similar volunteering experiences. But to be honest, as a fresh graduate, I don't have work experience in this field.

(6) Air China is domestically renowned for being highly internationalized in its passenger composition.

11. Master and practise.
SINGAPORE AIRLINES:

Flying Singapore Airlines can be a depressing experience because you may wish you could choose it on every route, domestic and international. Their excellence and consistency show just how good an airline can be and just how awful many US carriers really are. It is the first airline to take delivery of the new Airbus 380. Why is it considered the best airline in the world? Start with the newest, most sumptuous aircraft, ablus some of the best flight attendants, and food that can actually be memorable. While some say that economy on a Singapore flight is as good as Business on some carriers, we would rather say that travelers who fly Business or First on Singapore always seem to feel it was worth the price. Singapore now has competition from carriers like Emirates and Virgin Atlantic and loyalists claim that's a good thing. The entertainment menu, even in coach on the Airbus 340's, is far ahead of the competition but legroom in coach remains "tighter" than most would like. There are excellent connections in Singapore, home to one of the world's top three airports. Flaws are just hard to find and consistency and innovation continue to amaze those privileged enough to fly this carrier.

Overall Grade: A+

UNITED AIRLINES:

The sad fact is that United does not score at or near the top of any single category that matters to fliers with the exception of Star Alliance partners. Mileage can be used to upgrade on Lufthansa, SAS, US Air, and Singapore Airlines, among other Alliance partners. While the 777's that fly to London and Frankfurt get high marks out of Chicago, many grumble about the "ancient" 747's flying routes to the Orient. Seniority-based staff on international routes can seem to take their jobs for granted. Food and service in Business class does not compare to that offered by competing international carriers. Some fliers are willing to forget about poor in-flight service in lieu of UA's vast partner network and pilots who instill a high level of confidence. Experienced fliers choose Economy Plus seating which provides extra legroom at pricing just north of Economy.

Overall Grade: C

Answer Key

Unit 1 Pre-flight and Boarding

1. Warm-up: discuss in pairs and answer the following questions.

III. Complete the crossword puzzle with the given words and clues.
(1) lavatory   (2) demonstration   (3) luggage   (4) preflight   (5) earphone
(6) check   (7) greet   (8) direction   (9) cabin

2. Spot: what pre-flight tasks is the cabin crew in the picture doing?
(1) B   (2) A   (3) C   (4) D   (5) E   (6) F

7. Boarding announcements and safety checks.
A. fasten your seatbelt and tighten it adjust the seatback to the upright position
B. lift the window blind
C. tighten and fasten your seatbelt
D. Madam, would you please turn off the reading light?
E. Sir, would you please tow your bag under the seat in front of you?

8. Listen and learn.
(1)②   (2)①   (3)③   (4)④

12. Master and practise.

I. Listen to Sarah's interview and decide if the statement is true (T), false (F) or not mentioned (NM).
(1) F   (2) T   (3) T   (4) F   (5) T   (6) T   (7) T   (8) NM

II. Listen again and complete the passage below.
(1) preflight   (2) checking   (3) greet them   (4) sit down as soon as possible
(5) tell them where their seats locate   (6) get annoyed   (7) in the middle of the cabin

Unit 2 Routines after Take-off

1. Warm-up: discuss in pairs and answer the following questions.

III. Complete the crossword puzzle with the given words and clues.
(1) take off   (2) headrest   (3) blanket   (4) delay   (5) footrest

(6) secure   (7) boarding   (8) seatbelt   (9) laptop   (10) refreshment

2. Spot: categorize the passengers in the pictures with the given tags.
(1) F   (2) A   (3) D   (4) B   (5) E   (6) C

5. Complete the conversations with the words below.
① repeated   ② heated   ③ air-conditioner   ④ knob   ⑤ spare   ⑥ connection

6. Explore and learn: match the request during take-off with passenger's response.
(1) A②   (2) B①   (3) C⑥   (4) D③   (5) E⑤   (6) F④.

7. Language focus: describing problems.

II. Read the comments from passengers on a flight. Write sentences in two different ways using forms of the word in parentheses. Then compare with a partner.
(1) It's broken. There is some damage on it.
(2) It's stained. There is a stain on the cushion.
(3) This plastic cup is chipped. There is a chip on it.
(4) The one she is wearing is torn. It has a hole on the uniform she is wearing.

11. Master and practice.

I. Listen to the captain's announcement and complete the announcement during take-off.
(1) distance   (2) expected   (3) our airline

II. Listen to the purser giving further information to the passengers and complete the announcement.
(1) accordance   (2) smoking   (3) entertainment   (4) available   (5) call button
(6) meal   (7) trolleys

12. Read and think: Read the following passage and complete the tasks.
Task 2: Decide if the statement is true (T), false (F) or not mentioned (NM).
(1) T   (2) F   (3) NM   (4) T   (5) F

Unit 3 Passenger Comfort

1. Warm-up: Discuss in pairs and answer the following questions.

III. Complete the crossword puzzle with the given words and clues.
(1) compartment   (2) drop   (3) request   (4) problem   (5) baggage
(6) passenger   (7) arrival   (8) waste   (9) comfortable; cry

2. Spot: what is the problem the passenger(s) in each picture is having?
(1) F   (2) B   (3) D   (4) A   (5) E   (6) C

5. Understand passengers' requests.

I. What are the circled facilities in the picture? What problems/requests will the passengers have with these items?
  A. reading light   B. window blind   C. tray table
  D. overhead compartment   E. backrest   F. armrest
(1) A passenger might ask the flight attendant to fix the armrest.
(2) The flight attendant might ask a passenger to open/close the window blind.
(3) The flight attendant might ask a passenger to put back the tray table.
(4) A passenger might ask the flight attendant to open/close the overhead compartment.
(5) The flight attendant might ask a passenger to recline/adjust the backrest.
(6) The flight attendant might ask a passenger to switch off the reading light.

II. Why are the passengers in Picture 1 uncomfortable? What amenities do they need from Picture 2?
  A. Phoebe   B. Joey   C. Monica   D. Ross   E. Chandler
(1) Joey might be nauseous. He might ask for a waste bag.
(2) Monica might be thirsty. She might ask for water.
(3) Phoebe might be cold. She might ask for a blanket.
(4) Chandler might be bored. He might ask for newspaper.
(5) Ross might be hungry. He might ask for snacks.

6. Listen and learn.

I. Listen to the dialogues and number the pictures in order.
1②   2③   3①   4④

7. Explore and learn.
A (2)   B (5)   C (6)   D (1)   E (4)   F (3)

12. Master and practice:

I. Listen to the conversation and decide if the statement is true (T) or false (F).
(1) T   (2) F   (3) F   (4) T   (5) F   (6) F   (7) F   (8) T

II. Listen again and complete the passage below.
(1) buckle the seatbelt
(2) was sick
(3) take deep breaths
(4) bring a towel and some ice cubes

(5) place the towel on the forehead(and the back of her neck)
(6) the crying baby
(7) talk to the mother
(8) the teddy bear was lost
(9) go and have a look
(10) a teddy bear key chain
(11) have a look around

Unit 4 Food and Drink Service

1. Warm-up: discuss in pairs and answer the following questions.

III. Complete the crossword puzzle with the given words and clues.
(1) vegetarian   (2) mild   (3) alcohol   (4) choices   (5) trolley
(6) recommend   (7) menu   (8) tray   (9) spicy   (10) galley

2. Spot: match the food with the pictures.
(1) C   (2) A   (3) D   (4) E   (5) B   (6) F

5. Food on the meal tray.

I. Listen and label the objects on the meal tray.
(1) dessert/ ice-cream   (2) pure water   (3) bread   (4) salad   (5) fork
(6) chocolate   (7) butter   (8) knife   (9) spoon   (10) chicken curry with broccoli

II. Listen and complete the sentences.
(1) It's   (2) It's   (3) salted   (4) chocolate brownie   (5) want   (6) bowl

6. Serving drinks.

I. Which category do the listed belong to? Tick the category that matches the given drink.

Drink Menu	Alcohol	Soft Drinks	Hot Drinks
vodka	√		
Earl Grey tea			√
whisky	√		
coffee			√
rum	√		
coke		√	
espresso			√
champagne	√		

Drink Menu	Alcohol	Soft Drinks	Hot Drinks
lemonade		√	
sparkling water		√	
Seven Up		√	
Fanta		√	
fruit juice		√	
Sprite		√	
red wine	√		
peppermint tea			√
white wine	√		
cocktail	√		
hot chocolate			√
beer	√		
Martini	√		
black tea			√
gin and tonic	√		
green tea			√

7. Listen and learn.

I. Listen to the conversations. What does each passenger order and do they get what they want?

Passenger	Main course	Drinks	What they get
(1)	roasted chicken	a glass of whisky	roasted chicken a glass of whisky
(2)	beef	a glass of water	fish curry a glass of water
(3)	lasagna	apple juice	lasagna apple juice

II. Listen again and complete the phrases of offering and ordering food.

Offering Food

(1) Would you like something to eat?
(2) How about fish curry?
(3) May I offer you a drink, madam?
(4) What would you like to have for lunch, sir?

Making orders

(1) Do you have beef?
(2) Could I have a glass of pure water, please?

(3) Whisky on the rock, please.

(4) Black tea with milk, please.

Apologizing

(1) I'm sorry for having you waiting.

(2) I'm sorry that we've run out of the cheeseburger.

(3) I do apologize.

Giving the meal tray

(1) There you go, madam.

(2) Here you are, sir.

9. Making an apology.

I. Complete the conversation between a flight attendant and a passenger during the meal service.

(1) selection   (2) green tea   (3) sorry   (4) coffee   (5) turbulence
(6) terribly   (7) pain   (8) mind   (9) apologize   (10) another

11. Master and practise.

I. Listen and try to complete the announcement before meal service.

(1) fasten seatbelt   (2) cabin   (3) watch out   (4) put down   (5) choices
(6) vegetable   (7) dessert   (8) hot   (9) available   (10) pocket

II. Choose the best word or phrase to complete each sentence.

(1) B   (2) B   (3) B   (4) C   (5) B

12. Read and think: read the following passage and complete the tasks.

Task 2: Decide if the statement is true (T), false (F) or not mentioned (NM).

(1) F   (2) T   (3) T   (4) F   (5) T

Unit 5 Health and Medical Issues

1. Warm-up: discuss in pairs and answer the following questions.

III. Name the parts of the body with words from the box. Complete the crossword puzzle with the given words and clues.

(1) asthma   (2) bleeding   (3) wrist   (4) attack   (5) stomachache   (6) chest
(7) cramp   (8) ankle   (9) neck   (10) knee   (11) fever

2. Spot: what might be the issue with the passenger in each picture?

(1) E   (2) C   (3) D   (4) B   (5) F   (6) A

5. Identify passengers' conditions.

I. What is the passenger's condition? Match his/her description to the corresponding conditions in the answer box 2 and choose the right remedy for the passenger.

Conditions and remedies					
John	A	(1)	Jane	B	(4)
David	F	(2)	Alexander	E	(5)
Alice	C	(3)	April	D	(6)

II. Complete the sentences according to the given example.
Conversation (2)
①are you alright
②a cramp
③some tonic water and vitamin B
④I would suggest that

Conversation (3)
①Madam, are you alright
②get your daughter an inhaler and an oxygen mask

Conversation (4)
①Madam, are you alright
②get him some aspirin and perform a CPR

Conversation (5)
①Sir, are you alright
②get you a glass of salt water
③you do not have solid food for the time being

Conversation (6)
①Madam, are you alright
②get you a hot towel and some ice cubes
③you lie down and have a rest

6. Listen and learn.

I. Listen to the dialogues and number the pictures in order.
2② 4③ 3④ 1①

7. Explore and learn.
Conversation (1): I would suggest that

Conversation (2): I would suggest that
Conversation (3): You must
Conversation (4): I have to
Conversation (5): I'm afraid you have to

8. Write: fill in the blanks with appropriate responses and offers.
Situation Ⅰ
(1) I'll get you
(2) I would suggest that you

Situation Ⅱ
(1) I'll get you
(2) You must not

Situation Ⅲ
(1) I'll get you
(2) You must keep taking deep breaths

Situation Ⅳ
I'll help you lie down

12. Master and practise.

I. Listen to the conversation and decide if the statement is true(T), false(F) or not mentioned (NM).
(1) F   (2) T   (3) T   (4) NM   (5) NM   (6) T   (7) T   (8) NM

II. Listen again and complete the passage below.
(1) dizzy   (2) bleeding   (3) call a colleague   (4) had fainted
(5) help   (6) a physician   (7) perform the CPR

Unit 6 Safety and Emergency

1. Warm-up: discuss in pairs and answer the following questions.

III. Complete the crossword puzzle with the given words and clues.
(1) turbulence   (2) jacket   (3) emergency   (4) relax   (5) miracle
(6) grab   (7) loss   (8) decompression   (9) engine   (10) float

2. Spot: match the instruction A-F with the pictures.
(1) A   (2) B   (3) C   (4) D   (5) E   (6) F

5. Complete the conversation using the words below.
(1) upset　(2) experiencing　(3) life jacket　(4) located　(5) tab
(6) straps　(7) inflate　(8) aircraft　(9) whistle　(10) attention

6. Give instructions about dos and don'ts.

I. Match the verbs with the phrases to complete the instructions used in emergencies.
A (6)　B(8)　C(4)　D (9)　E (5)　F (10)　G (1)　H (7)　I(2)　J(3)

7. Listen and learn.

I. Listen to the conversations and mark the sentences True (T) or False (F).
Conversation (1): ①T　②T
Conversation (2): ①F　②T
Conversation (3): ①F　②T

II. Listen again and complete the sentences.
(1) switched　(2) must　(3) went off　(4) lavatory　(5) bumpy　(6) ensure

8. Explore and learn: in all emergencies, cabin crew must give the information and instructions to reassure the passengers. Match the concerns of passengers and the proper response.
A(2)　B(1)　C(3)　D(6)　E(4)　F(5)

9. Language focus: time clauses.

I. Reorder the words to make sentences.
(1) Don't inflate the life jacket until you leave the cabin.
(2) We'll be serving meals after half an hour.
(3) You can move around the cabin once the fasten seatbelt sign is off.
(4) Remain seated until the aircraft stops.

12. Master and practise.

I. Listen and try to complete the announcement under emergency.
(1) emergency　(2) pressure　(3) fastened　(4) automatically　(5) pull
(6) elastic band　(7) normally　(8) mask　(9) panic　(10) informed

13. Read and think: read the following passage and complete the tasks.
Task 2: Decide if the statement is true (T), false (F) or not mentioned (NM).
(1) F　(2) T　(3) F　(4) T　(5) T

Unit 7 Descent, Landing and Layover

1. Warm-up: discuss in pairs and answer the following questions.

III. Complete the crossword puzzle with the given words and clues.
(1) arrival   (2) landing   (3) shuttle; stow   (4) warn   (5) approximately
(6) ensure   (7) cruise   (8) descent   (9) taxiing

2. Spot: match the sentences A-F with the pictures.
(1) C   (2) B   (3) E   (4) F   (5) D   (6) A

5. Complete the conversation using the words below.
(1) landing   (2) stow   (3) tray   (4) pass   (5) adjust   (6) armrest

6. Before landing flight attendants will make final checks.

II. Look at the situations below and use the verbs in the brackets to make polite requests.
(1) Please stow the tray table.
(2) Please switch off the iPad.
(3) Please put up the seatback.
(4) Please buckle up the seatbelt.
(5) Please put away the carry-on baggage.
(6) Please fill in the immigration form.

7. Listen and learn.

I. Listen to the conversations and mark the sentences True (T) or False (F).
Conversation (1): ①T ②F
Conversation (2): ①T ②F
Conversation (3): ①T ②T

II. Listen and complete the sentences.
(1) closed   (2) arriving   (3) local   (4) check   (5) cellphone   (6) second

8. Explore and learn: permission, obligation and prohibition.

I. Match these rules with the correct sign.
(1) ①   (2) ③   (3) ②   (4) ④

9. Language focus: study the phrases verbs with pronouns.

I. Rewrite the instruction using a pronoun instead of the noun.
(1) Please switch it off.
(2) Please fold it away.
(3) Please stow them in the overhead compartment.
(4) Please turn it off immediately.
(5) Please open it.
(6) Please put it down.

11. Master and practise.

I. Listen and try to complete the pre-landing announcement.
(1) apologize   (2) switched on   (3) remain   (4) overhead compartment   (5) stowed
(6) switched off   (7) lavatories   (8) entertainment   (9) landing   (10) headsets

12. Read and think.
Task 2: Decide if the statement is true (T), false (F) or not mentioned (NM).
(1) T   (2) T   (3) NM   (4) T   (5) F

Unit 8   Getting a Job

1. Warm-up: discuss in pairs and answer the following questions.

III. Complete the crossword puzzle with the given words and clues.
(1) personality   (2) quality   (3) airline   (4) interest   (5) interview
(6) introduce   (7) experience   (8) strength   (9) hobby   (10) difficulty

2. Spot: match the interview question with the answer.
(1) F   (2) D   (3) C   (4) E   (5) A   (6) B

6. Listen and learn: expressing opinions.

I. Listen to the dialogues and number the pictures in order.
3①   1②   4④   2③

12. Master and practice:

I. Listen to the conversation and decide if the statement is true (T) or false (F).
(1) F   (2) F   (3) T   (4) T   (5) T   (6) F   (7) T   (8) T

II. Listen again and complete the passage below.
(1) Singapore Airlines and United Airlines

(2) is better
(3) good services
(4) take delivery of the new Airbus 380
(5) flight attendants
(6) entertainment menu
(7) the legroom is tighter
(8) Star Alliance
(9) take their jobs for granted
(10) does not compare to
(11) extra legroom

参 考 文 献

[1] Terence Gerighty, Shon Davis, 陈方.空乘英语[M].上海：上海外语教育出版社, 2023.
[2] Sue Ellis, Lewis Lansford.Enlish for Cabin Crew[M].牛津：牛津大学出版社, 2014.
[3] 范建一.民航乘务英语实用会话[M].北京：中国民航出版社, 2018.